BIRDS
THROUGH AN
OPERA-GLASS

BIRDS

THROUGH AN OPERA-GLASS

BY

FLORENCE A. MERRIAM

APPLEWOOD BOOKS

Birds Through an Opera-Glass was originally published in 1889
by Houghton, Mifflin and Company. This publication is a
facsimile of the 1890 edition published by Chautauqua Press.

Published by Applewood Books,
an imprint of Arcadia Publishing

ISBN 978-1-4290-9569-3

For a complete list of books currently available,
please visit us at www.applewoodbooks.com

MANUFACTURED IN CHINA

INTRODUCTION

WHEREVER there are people there are birds, so it makes comparatively little difference where you live, if you are only in earnest about getting acquainted with your feathered neighbors. Even in a Chicago back yard fifty-seven kinds of birds have been seen in a year, and in a yard in Portland, Connecticut, ninety-one species have been recorded. Twenty-six kinds are known to nest in the city of Washington, and in the parks and cemeteries of San Francisco in winter I have found twenty-two kinds, while seventy-six are recorded for Prospect Park, Brooklyn, and a hundred and forty-two for Central Park, New York.

There are especial advantages in beginning to study birds in the cities, for by going to the museums you can compare the bird skins with the birds you have seen in the field. And, moreover, you can get an idea of the grouping of the different families which will help you materially in placing the live bird when you meet him at home.

If you do not live in the city, as I have said elsewhere, " shrubby village dooryards, the trees of village streets, and orchards, roadside fences, overgrown pastures, and the borders of brooks and rivers are among the best places to look for birds." [1]

When going to watch birds, " provided with opera-glass and note-book, and dressed in inconspicuous colors, proceed to some good birdy place, — the bushy bank of a stream or an old juniper pasture, — and sit down in the undergrowth or against a concealing tree-trunk, with your back to the sun, to look and listen in silence. You will be able to trace most songs to their singers by finding which tree the song comes from, and then watching for *movement*, as birds are rarely motionless long at a time when singing. It will be a help if, besides writing a careful description of both bird and song, you draw a rough diagram of the bird's markings, and put down the actual notes of his song as nearly as may be.

" If you have time for only a walk through the woods, go as quietly as possible and stop often, listening to catch the notes which your footsteps have drowned. Timid birds may often be attracted by answering their calls, for it is very reassuring to be addressed in one's native tongue." [2]

Birds' habits differ in different localities, and as this book was written in the East, many birds are spoken of as common which Western readers will find rare or wanting; but nearly the same

[1] *Birds of Village and Field.*

[2] Maynard's *Birds of Washington.* Introduction by F. A. M.

families of birds are found in all parts of the United States, so that, if not able to name your bird exactly, at least you will be able to tell who his relatives are.

Boys who are interested in watching the coming of the birds from the south in spring, and their return from·the north in the fall, can get blank migration schedules by applying to the Biological Survey, Department of Agriculture, Washington, D. C.; and teachers and others who want material for bird work can get, free on application, the publications of the Biological Survey, which show how the food of birds affects the farm and garden. Much additional information can be obtained from the secretaries of the State Audubon Societies, and their official organ, "Bird-Lore."

Photography is coming to hold an important place in nature work, as its notes cannot be questioned, and the student who goes afield armed with opera-glass and camera will not only add more to our knowledge than he who goes armed with a gun, but will gain for himself a fund of enthusiasm and a lasting store of pleasant memories. For more than all the statistics is the sanity and serenity of spirit that comes when we step aside from the turmoil of the world to hold quiet converse with Nature.

FLORENCE A. MERRIAM.

Washington, D. C., May 11, 1899.

CONTENTS.

WARBLERS.

APPENDIX.

BIRDS THROUGH AN OPERA-GLASS.

We are so in the habit of focusing our spy-glasses on our human neighbors that it seems an easy matter to label them and their affairs, but when it comes to birds, — alas! not only are there legions of kinds, but, to our bewildered fancy, they look and sing and act exactly alike. Yet though our task seems hopeless at the outset, before we recognize the conjurer a new world of interest and beauty has opened before us.

The best way is the simplest. Begin with the commonest birds, and train your ears and eyes by pigeon-holing every bird you see and every song you hear. Classify roughly at first, — the finer distinctions will easily be made later. Suppose, for instance, you are in the fields on a spring morning. Standing still a moment, you hear what sounds like a confusion of songs. You think you can never tell one from another, but by listening carefully you at once notice a difference. Some are true songs, with a definite melody, — and tune, if one may use that word, — like the song of several of the sparrows, with three high notes and a run

down the scale. Others are only monotonous
trills, always the same two notes, varying only in
length and intensity, such as that of the chipping
bird, who makes one's ears fairly ache as he sits
in the sun and trills to himself, like a complacent
prima donna. Then there is always plenty of gos-
siping going on, chippering and chattering that
does not rise to the dignity of song, though it adds
to the general jumble of sounds ; but this should
be ignored at first, and only the loud songs listened for. When the trill and the elaborate song
are once contrasted, other distinctions are easily
made. The ear then catches the quality of songs.
On the right the plaintive note of the meadow-
lark is heard, while out of the grass at the left
comes the rollicking song of the bobolink.

Having begun sorting sounds, you naturally
group sights, and so find yourself parceling out
the birds by size and color. As the robin is a
well-known bird, he serves as a convenient unit
of measure — an ornithological foot. If you call
anything from a humming-bird to a robin small,
and from a robin to a crow large, you have a
practical division line, of use in getting your
bearings. And the moment you give heed to colors, the birds will no longer look alike. To sim-
plify matters, the bluebird, the oriole with his
orange and black coat, the scarlet tanager with
his flaming plumage, and all the other bright birds
can be classed together ; while the sparrows, fly-

catchers, thrushes, and vireos may be thought of as the dull birds.

When the crudest part of the work is done, and your eye and ear naturally seize differences of size, color, and sound, the interesting part begins. You soon learn to associate the birds with fixed localities, and once knowing their favorite haunts, quickly find other clues to their ways of life.

By going among the birds, watching them closely, comparing them carefully, and writing down, while in the field, all the characteristics of every new bird seen, — its locality, size, color, details of marking, song, food, flight, eggs, nest, and habits, — you will come easily and naturally to know the birds that are living about you. The first law of field work is *exact observation*, but not only are you more likely to observe accurately if what you see is put in black and white, but you will find it much easier to identify the birds from your notes than from memory.

With these hints in mind, go to look for your friends. Carry a pocket note-book, and above all, take an opera or field glass with you. Its rapid adjustment may be troublesome at first, but it should be the "inseparable article" of a careful observer. If you begin work in spring, don't start out before seven o'clock, because the confusion of the matins is discouraging — there is too much to see and hear. But go as soon as possible after breakfast, for the birds grow quiet and fly to the woods for their nooning earlier and earlier as the weather gets warmer.

You will not have to go far to find your first bird.

I.

THE ROBIN.

NEXT to the crow, the robin is probably our best known bird ; but as a few of his city friends have never had the good fortune to meet him, and as he is to be our " unit of measure," it behooves us to consider him well. He is, as every one knows, a domestic bird, with a marked bias for society. Everything about him bespeaks the self-respecting American citizen. He thinks it no liberty to dine in your front yard, or build his house in a crotch of your piazza, with the help of the string you have inadvertently left within reach. Accordingly, he fares well, and keeps fat on cherries and straw-berries if the supply of fish-worms runs low. Mr. Robin has one nervous mannerism — he jerks his tail briskly when excited. But he is not always looking for food as the woodpeckers appear to be, nor flitting about with nervous restlessness like the warblers, and has, on the whole, a calm, dignified air. With time to meditate when he chooses, like other sturdy, well-fed people, his reflections usually take a cheerful turn ; and when he lapses into a poetical mood, as he often does at sunrise and

sunset, sitting on a branch in the softened light
and whispering a little song to himself, his senti-
ment is the wholesome every-day sort, with none
of the sadness or longing of his cousins, the
thrushes, but full of contented appreciation of the
beautiful world he lives in.

Unlike some of his human friends, his content
does not check his activity.   He is full of buoyant
life.   He may always be heard piping up above
the rest of the daybreak chorus, and I have seen
him sit on top of a stub in a storm when it seemed
as if the harder it rained the louder and more ju-
bilantly he sang.   He has plenty of pluck and
industry, too, for every season he dutifully accepts
the burden of seeing three or four broods of bird
children through all the dangers of cats, hawks,

and first flights : keeping successive nestfuls of gaping mouths supplied with worms all the summer through.

His red breast is a myth and belongs to his English namesake ; and it must be owned that his is a homely reddish brown that looks red only when the sunlight falls on it. His wife's breast is even less red than his — in fact, she looks as if the rain had washed off most of her color. But, perhaps, had they been beautiful they would have been vain, and then. alas for the robins we know and love now. When the children make their debut, they are more strikingly homely than their parents ; possibly because we have known the old birds until, like some of our dearest friends, their plainness has become beautiful to us. In any case, the eminently speckled young gentlemen that come out with their new tight-fitting suits and awkward ways do not meet their father's share of favor.

Perhaps the nest they come from accounts for their lack of polish. It is compact and strong, built to last, and to keep out the rain ; but with no thought of beauty. In building their houses the robins do not follow our plan, but begin with the frame and work in. When the twigs and weed stems are securely placed they put on the plaster — a thick layer of mud that the bird moulds with her breast till it is as hard and smooth as a plaster cast. And inside of all, for cleanliness and comfort. they lay a soft lining of dried grass. This is the typical nest, but of course, there are marked variations from it. Usually it is firmly fixed in the crotch of a branch or close to the body of the tree where its weight can be supported.

But who does not know instances of oddly placed nests outside of trees? The "American Naturalist" records one "on the top of a long pole, which stood without support in an open barnyard," and Audubon notes one within a few feet of a blacksmith's anvil. A number of interesting sites have come within my notice. Among them are: the top of a blind; an eave trough; a shingle that projected over the inner edge of an open shed; and, most singular of all, one inside a milk-house, set precariously on the rim of a barrel that lay on its side, just above the heads of the men who not only appeared both night and morning with alarmingly big milk pails, but made din enough in plying a rattling creaky pump handle to have sent any ordinary bird bolting through the window.

Robins usually nest comparatively high, though Audubon tells of a nest found on a bare rock on the ground, and this summer I found one in the crotch of a small tree only two and a half feet from the earth. It was near a hen yard, so perhaps Madam Robin was following the fashion by laying her eggs near the ground. In any case, she was on visiting terms with the hen-roost, for, singularly enough, there were feathers plastered about the adobe wall, though none inside.   Perhaps the weather was too warm for a feather bed! — or was this frivolous lady bird thinking so much of fashion and adornment she could spare no time on homely comfort?

Longfellow says :

"There are no birds in last year's nest,"

but on a brace in an old cow shed I know of, there is a robin's nest that has been used for several years.   A layer of new material has been added to the old structure each time, so that it is now eight inches high and bids fair soon to rival the fourteen story flat houses of New York.   A remarkable case is given in the "Naturalist" of a robin that had no "bump of locality," and distributed its building material impartially over nearly thirty feet of the outer cornice of a house.

You may look for robins almost anywhere, but they usually prefer dry open land, or the edge of woodland, being averse to the secluded life of their relatives, the thrushes, who build in the forest.   Those I find in the edge of the woods are much shyer than those living about the house, probably from the same reason that robins and others of our most friendly Eastern birds are wild and suspicious in the uninhabited districts of the West — or, who will say there are no recluses among birds as well as men?

The flight and song of the robin are characteristic.   The flight is rapid, clear cut, and straight.

Unlike many birds, he moves as if he were going somewhere. His voice is a strong clear treble, loud and cheerful, but he is not a musician, and has no one set song. His commonest call has two parts, each of three notes run together ; the first with a rising, the last with a falling inflection, like, *tril-la-ree, tril-la-rah ; tril-la-ree, tril-la-rah.* But he has a number of calls, and you must be familiar with the peculiar treble quality of his note to avoid confusing it with others.

In the fall, Lowell says,

> "The sobered robin hunger-silent now,
> Seeks cedar-berries blue, his autumn cheer,"

and this "sobered" suggests a question. Why is it that as soon as robins form flocks, they become shy? Is it because they are more often shot at when migrating in large numbers ; or because, as Mr. William Hubbell Fisher suggests, they have left their homes, and so have lost confidence in the surroundings and people ?

In some localities they live on cedar-berries in the fall, but here they are well satisfied with mountain ash berries, wild cherries, and ungathered crab apples. Speaking of their food, what a pity that anglers cannot contract with them for a supply of bait! Woe betide the fish-worm that stirs the grass on the lawn within their hearing! How wise they look as they cock their heads on one side and stand, erect and motionless, peering down on the ground. And what a surprise it

must be to the poor worm when they suddenly tip
forward, give a few rapid hops, and diving into
the grass drag him out of his retreat.   Though
they run from a chicken, robins will chase chip-
munks and fight with red squirrels in defense of
their nests or young.

II.

THE CROW.

THE despised crow is one of our most interesting birds.   His call is like the smell of the brown
furrows in spring — life is more sound and wholesome for it.   Though the crow has no song, what
a variety of notes and tones he can boast!   In
vocabulary, he is a very Shakespeare among birds.
Listening to a family of Frenchmen, though you
do not know a word of French, you easily guess
the temper and drift of their talk, and so it is in
listening to crows — tone, inflection, gesture, all
betray their secrets.   One morning last October
I caught, in this way, a spicy chapter in crow family discipline.

I was standing in a meadow of rich aftermath
lying between a stony pasture and a small piece
of woods, when a young crow flew over my head,
cawing softly to himself.   He flew straight west
toward the pasture for several seconds, and then,
as if an idea had come to him, turned his head

and neck around in the intelligent crow fashion,
circled back to the woods, lit, and cawed vocifer-
ously to three other crows till they came over
across the pasture.

After making them all circle over my head, per-
haps·merely as a blind, he took them back to his
perch where he wanted them to go beechnutting
— or something else. Whatever it was, they evidently scorned his childishness, for they flew back
to their tree across the field as fast as they had
come. This put him in a pet, and he would not
budge, but sat there sputtering like a spoiled
child. To everything he said, whether in a complaining or teasing tone, the same gruff paternal
caw came back from the pasture. " Come along ! "
it seemed to say. To this the refractory son would
respond, " I won't." They kept it up for several
minutes, but at last paternal authority conquered,
and the big boy, making a wide detour, flew slowly
and reluctantly back to his family. He lit on a
low branch under them, and when the father gave
a gruff " I should think it was time you came," he
defiantly shook his tail and cleaned his bill. After
a few moments he condescended to make a low
half sullen, half subdued remark, but when the
family all started off again he sat and scolded
some time before he would follow them, and I
suspect he compromised matters then only because
he did not want to be left behind.

The " intelligence of the crow " has become a

platitude, but when we hear of his cracking clams by dropping them on a fence, coming to roost with the hens in cold weather, and — in the case of a tame crow — opening a door by lighting on the latch, his originality is a surprise. A family near here had much merriment over the gambols of a pet crow named Jim. Whenever he saw the gardener passing to and fro between the house and garden, he would fly down from the trees, light on his hat, and ride back and forth. He liked to pick the bright blossoms, particularly pansies and scarlet geraniums, and would not only steal bright colored worsteds and ribbons, but tear all the yellow covers from any novels he came across. When any one went to the vegetable garden he showed the most commendable eagerness to help with the work, being anxious to pick whatever was wanted — from raspberries and currants to the little cucumbers gathered for pickling.

The sight of the big black puppy waddling along wagging high in air a long black tail incongruously finished off with a tipping of white hairs was too much for Jim's sobriety. Down he would dive, give a nip at the hairs, and be gravely seated on a branch just out of reach by the time Bruno had turned to snap at him. Let the puppy move on a step, and down the mischief would come again, and so the two would play — sometimes for more than half an hour at a time. Then again, the joke would take a more practical turn, for, in-

stead of flying overhead when Bruno looked back,
Jim would steal the bone the puppy had been
gnawing.

The crow was happy as long as any one would
play with him, and never tired of flying low over
the ground with a string dangling from his bill for
the children to run after. Another favorite play
was to hold on to a string or small stick with his
bill while some one lifted him up by it, as a baby
is tossed by its arms. He would even hold on and
let you " swing him around your head." He was
never daunted, and when the toddling two-year-
old would get too rough in her play and strike at
him with her stick, he would either catch the hem
of her pinafore and hold on till she ran away, or
would try scaring her, rushing at her — his big
black wings spread out and his bill wide open.

One day his pluck was thoroughly tested.
Hearing loud caws of distress coming from the
lawn, the gardener rushed across and found Jim
lying on his back, his claw tightly gripping the
end of one of the wings of a large hawk, that,
surprised and terrified by this turn of the tables
was struggling frantically to get away. Jim held
him as tight as a vise, and only loosened his grasp
to give his enemy into the gardener's hands. After
letting go he submitted to the victor's reward, letting his wounds be examined and his bravery ex-
tolled while he was carried about — wearing a
most consciously heroic air, it must be confessed
— for due celebration of the victory.

III.

THE BLUEBIRD.

As you stroll through the meadows on a May morning, drinking in the spring air and sunshine, and delighting in the color of the dandelions and the big bunches of blue violets that dot the grass, a bird call comes quavering overhead that seems the voice of all country loveliness. Simple, sweet, and fresh as the spirit of the meadows, with a tinge of forest richness in the plaintive *tru-al-ly* that marks the rhythm of our bluebird's undulating flight, wherever the song is heard, from city street or bird-box, it must bring pictures of flowering fields, blue skies, and the freedom of the wandering summer winds.

Look at the bluebird now as he goes over your head — note the cinnamon of his breast; and as he flies down and turns quickly to light on the fence post, see the cobalt-blue that flashes from his back. These colors are the poet's signs that the bird's sponsors are the " earth and sky." And the little creature has a wavering way of lifting its wings when perching, as if hesitating between earth and sky, that may well carry out the poet's hint of his wild ethereal spirit.

Notice the bluebird's place in literature. The robin, with his cheerful soprano call, serves as the emblem of domestic peace and homely cheer; but the bluebird, with his plaintive contralto warble, stirs the imagination, and is used as the poetic symbol of spring. The temper of the bluebird makes him a fit subject for the poet's encomiums. Mr. Burroughs goes so far as to say that "the expression of his indignation is nearly as musical as his song."

Lowell speaks of the bluebird as

> " shifting his light load of song
> From post to post along the cheerless fence."

But although he is as restless and preoccupied here as elsewhere, lifting his wings tremulously as if in reality "shifting his load of song," and longing to fly away, the bluebird sometimes comes down to the prose of life even here and actually hides his nest in the hole of a fence rail. When this is not his fancy he fits up an old woodpecker's hole in a post, stub, or tree; or, if more social in his habits, builds in knot-holes in the sides of barns, or in bird-boxes arranged for his use. At Northampton I was shown a nest in an old stub by the side of the road, so shallow that the father and mother birds fed their young from the outside, clinging to the sides of the hole and reaching in to drop the food into the open mouths below.

Although the bluebird has such a model temper, it has not always a clear idea of the laws of meum and tuum, as was shown by a nest found directly on top of a poor swallow's nest where there lay four fresh eggs! The nest is usually lined with dry grasses and similar materials. The eggs, from four to seven in number, are generally plain pale greenish blue, but occasionally white.

Sitting on a fence at a little distance the young birds look almost black, but as they fly off you catch a tinge of blue on their wings and tails. Their mother is more like her husband, but, as with most lady birds, her tints are subdued — doubtless the result of "adaptation," as bright colors on the back of the brooding mother would attract danger.

We have two reasons for gratitude to the blue-bird. It comes home early in the spring, and is among the last to leave in the fall, its sweet note trembling on the air when the "bare branches of the trees are rattling in the wind."

IV.

CHIMNEY SWIFT; CHIMNEY "SWALLOW."

WATCH a chimney swift as he comes near you, rowing through the air first with one wing and then the other, or else cruising along with sails set. Look at him carefully and you will see that he is not a swallow, although he often goes by that name. He looks much more like a bat. His outlines are so clear cut and angular that he could be reduced, roughly, to two triangles, their common base cutting his body vertically in halves.

His tail is, of itself, an acute-angled triangle terminating merely in bristles; and his wings look as if made of skin stretched on a frame, bat fashion, instead of being of feathers.

He twitters in a sharp chippering way as he flutters through the air and picks up flies, saying, as Mr. Burroughs puts it, "chippy-chippy-chirio, not a man in Dario can catch a chippy-chippy-chirio." And you are inclined to believe the boast — such zigzag darting, such circling and running! The men of Dario would need seven league wings to keep up with him, and then, after a lightning race, when just ready to throw their pinch of salt, with a sudden wheel the chippy-chirio would dart down a chimney and disappear from sight.

And what a noise these swifts do make in the chimneys! If you ever had a room beside one of their lodging-houses you can testify to their "nocturnal habits during the nesting season." Such chattering and jabbering, such rushing in and scrambling out! If you only could get your spyglass inside the chimney! Their curious little nests are glued against the sides like tiny wall pockets; and there the swifts roost, or rather hang, clinging to the wall, side by side, like little sooty bats. Audubon says that before the young birds are strong enough to fly they clamber up to the mouths of the chimneys as the pitifully triumphant chimney-sweeps used to come up for a breath and wave their brooms in the air at their escape from the dangers below. Though never venturing near us the swifts come to live inside our houses. Like the robin they are citizens, but what a contrast !

Their feet are weak from disuse, and it is believed that they never light anywhere except in a chimney or in a hollow tree, where they sometimes go at night and in bad weather. They gather the twigs they glue together for their nests while on the wing, and their ingenuity in doing it shows how averse they are to lighting. Audubon says : " The chimney swallows are seen in great numbers whirling around the tops of some decayed or dead tree, as if in pursuit of their insect prey. Their movements at this time are exceedingly rapid; they throw their body suddenly against the twig, grapple it with their feet, and by an instantaneous jerk snap it off short, and proceed with it to the place intended for the nest."

V.

CATBIRD.

HIGH trees have an unsocial aspect, and so, as Lowell says, " The catbird croons in the lilac-bush," in the alders, in a prickly ash copse, a barberry-bush, or by the side of the garden. In Northampton one of his favorite haunts is an old

orchard that slopes down to the edge of Mill
River. Here he is welcomed every year by his
college girl friends; and in the open seclusion of
an apple-tree proceeds to build his nest and raise
his little family, singing through it all with keen
enjoyment of the warm sunshine and his own company.

To the tyro the catbird is at once the most interesting and most exasperating of birds. Like
some people, he seems to give up his time to the
pleasure of hearing himself talk. A first cousin
of the mocking-bird — whom he resembles in person much more than in voice — perhaps the relationship accounts for his overweening confidence
in his vocal powers. As a matter of fact his jerky
utterance is so harsh that it has been aptly termed
asthmatic.

The catbird is unmistakably a Bohemian. He
is exquisitely formed, and has a beautiful slate-
gray coat, set off by his black head and tail. By
nature he is peculiarly graceful, and when he
chooses can pass for the most polished of the
Philistine aristocracy. But he cares nothing for
all this. With lazy self-indulgence he sits by the
hour with relaxed muscles, and listlessly drooping
wings and tail. If he were a man you feel confident that he would sit in shirt sleeves at home
and go on the street without a collar.

And his occupation? His cousin is an artist,
but he — is he a wag as well as a caricaturist, or

is he in sober earnest when he tries to mimic the inimitable Wilson's thrush? If a wag he is a success, for he deceives the unguarded into believing him a robin, a cat, and — "a bird new to science!" How he must chuckle over the enthusiasm which hails his various notes and the bewilderment and chagrin that come to the diligent observer who finally catches a glimpse of the garrulous mimic!

The catbird builds his nest as he does everything else. The loose mass of coarse twigs patched up with pieces of newspaper or anything he happens to fancy, looks as if it would hardly bear his weight. He lines it, however, with fine bits of brown and black roots, and when the beautiful dark green eggs are laid in it, you feel sure that such an artistic looking bird must enjoy the contrasting colors.

VI.

KEEL - TAILED BLACKBIRD; CROW BLACKBIRD; BRONZED GRACKLE.

LOWELL gives this bird the first place in the calendar. He says : —

> "Fust come the blackbirds clatt'rin' in tall trees,
> And settlin' things in windy Congresses, —
> Queer politicians, though, for I 'll be skinned
> If all on 'em don't head against the wind."

In spite of all that may be brought up in Grand

Jury against these "queer politicians," who is there that could not confess to a thrill of pleasure when they appear about the house "clatt'rin' in tall trees"?

As Mr. Burroughs has it: "The air is filled with cracking, splintering, spurting, semi-musical sounds, which are like pepper and salt to the ear." There is a delicious reality to their notes. We feel now that spring is not a myth of the poets, after all, but that she has sent this black advance guard as a promise of wild flowers and May-day.

Black, did I say? Nothing could be more misleading. Mr. Ridgway describes the body of the purple grackle as "brassy olive or bronze," his neck as "steel-blue, violet, purple, or brassy green," and his wings and tail as "purplish or violet-purplish." He is one of the most brilliant of our bird beauties. Watch him as he ambles over the branches, and when the sunlight strikes him you will wonder who could have been so blind as to dub him blackbird. Call him, rather, the black opal!

He is a bird of many accomplishments. To begin with, he does not condescend to hop, like ordinary birds, but imitates the crow in his stately walk; then he has a steering apparatus that the small boy might well study in coasting time. He can turn his tail into a rudder. Watch him as he flies. While is going straight ahead you do not notice anything unusual, but as soon as he turns or wants to alight you see his tail change from the horizontal to the vertical — into a rudder. He is called keel-tailed on account of it.

Moreover, he can pick beechnuts, catch crayfish without getting nipped, and fish for minnows alongside of any ten-year-old. Last October I found him beech-nutting, but he made hard work of it. I suspect the cold snap — for there was snow on the ground — had stiffened his toes so that he was more awkward than usual. Poor fellow, I felt sorry for him, it entailed such dangerous gymnastics! But it was amusing to see him walk over the branches, stretch his neck to the point of dislocation, and then make such a determined dive after the nut that he nearly lost his balance, and could only save himself by a desperate jerk of the tail. Even when he picked out a nut he had to put it under his claw and drill through the shell, pick-axe style, before he could get a morsel to eat. He evidently thought it rather serious sport, and flew down for some shriveled crab-apples as a second course. But an army of robins had possession of the apple-tree and two of them were detailed to drive him off, so he had to finish his breakfast up in the cold beech top.

A long list of nesting sites might be given, including martin-houses, poplars, evergreens, holes in stubs, the sides of fish hawk's nests, and church spires where the blackbirds' "clatt'rin'" is drowned by the tolling bells. Instances of their quarrels with robins and other birds would fill a volume, but the most interesting feud of which I have heard was enacted in the garden of the keen observer and botanist, Mrs. Helen M. Bagg, and its progress was watched by her unnoticed, as she looked out upon the participants from among the flowering shrubs and vines that surround her cottage. I quote her racy description : —

"Early one May two robins, with many manifestations of happiness, set up house-keeping in a tree near the south end of my house. A few days later a large flock of blackbirds alighted on the trees on the north side of the yard. There had been a blackbird wedding, and their friends had escorted them hither with the laudable intention of finding a suitable location for a nest for the happy pair. A loud chattering and fluttering followed, one advising this place, another that. At length the young husband espied the broad top of the water-pipe, under the eaves, and settled on that as a most secure and suitable home for his bride. The wedding guests, with the satisfaction that comes from the consciousness of having performed one's duty, took their departure, leaving the blissful couple to the uninterrupted enjoyment of their own society. Ah! who could have foretold 'on night so fair, such awful morn' could rise?"

" In the mean time the robins had been watching these unusual proceedings with much anxiety and uneasiness ; apparently not well pleased and not a little alarmed that their hereditary foes should presume to invade their domains and become domiciled in such close proximity to their own residence. But they made no hostile demonstrations that day, waiting to see the turn of affairs, and, as the sequel shows, to gain time to summon the assistance of friends. Early the next morning they resolved to eject the new-comers from the premises.

" Then occurred the most remarkable scene I ever witnessed. At the loud cries of the combatants an immense number of birds of both kinds came flocking from all quarters to the scene of action, as if they had been expecting the affray. They attacked each other with great ferocity and fought pluckily with bills and feet amid loud cries of anger and derision. Feathers flew. The wounded would fly away to a neighboring tree to nurse their hurts for a moment, when, still smarting with pain, back they would come to fight with redoubled fury. The shrieks and cries increased till it seemed a veritable pandemonium. Every robin and blackbird within the radius of a mile must have been present, either as spectator or participant in the strife. After a time, finding that both parties were equally brave, and that neither would yield, they with one accord withdrew from the conflict as suddenly as they came, a few only remaining to arbitrate matters.

" The path from the house to the road divides the yard into equal parts. It was agreed that in future the blackbirds should keep on the north side, and the robins on the south side of this path. Peace and quiet reigned the rest of the day, all parties being too exhausted to resume the struggle even if they had not been in honor bound to respect the treaty. But do not fancy that the feud was forgotten. By no means. The sleek black-coated, dapper young gentleman, conscious of having won the victory, inasmuch as he had not been dislodged from his position, allowed no opportunity to pass in which he might show his contempt for or exult over his plainly-dressed and comparatively inelegant neighbors.

" When the nest-building commenced, our gay chevalier complacently permitted his meek little wife to perform the main part of the labor, while he would perch himself on a limb as near the dividing line as possible and taunt or ridicule his opponents, whom family cares alone prevented from reciprocating the compliments — the will and desire were strong enough. Sometimes he would examine the nest to see how the work progressed, and occasionally he condescended to pick up a straw and fly with it to a tree near by, and sit there with it in his mouth with a wonderfully self-satisfied air, yet never offering it to his mate.

After a few moments he would drop it, smooth his plumage, wheel about, whisk his tail, and perform various other antics for the delectation of Mrs. Blackbird ; then he would suddenly dart off to see what the robins were about.

" During the weeks that followed, through nest-making and incubation, the enmity between the blackbirds and robins never abated. They were ever wary and on the alert, and if it chanced that either party, returning to his home, happened to cross the ' Mason and Dixon's line,' the other was out of his nest in a trice to drive off the intruder. Sometimes I thought both parties courted these occasions, though they would generally content themselves with angry words and looks. The next year they, or their children, returned, and each took amicable possession of his old nesting-place, neither deigning to notice his neighbor."

VII.

BOBOLINK; REED-BIRD; RICE-BIRD.

THOUGH the bluebird brings the poet pictures of fields blooming with dandelions and blue violets, and visions of all the freshness and beauty of nature, it tinges his thought with the tremulous sadness and longing of spring; but Robert o' Lincoln, the light-hearted laugher of June, brings him the spirit of the long bright days when the sun streams full upon meadows glistening with buttercups and daisies.

Pray, have you seen the merry minstrel singing over the fields, or sitting atilt of a grass stem? And do you know what an odd dress he masquerades in? If not, let me warn you. One day at college some young observers came to me in great excitement. They had seen a new bird. It was a marvelous, unheard-of creature — its back was white and its breast black. What could it be? Later on, when we were out one day, a bobolink flew on to the campus. That was their bird. And to justify their description they exclaimed, " He looks as if his clothes were turned around." And so he does.

Shades of short hair and bloomers, what an innovation! How the birds must gossip! Instead of the light-colored shirt and vest and decorous dark coat sanctioned by the Worth of conven-

tional bird circles for centuries, this radical decks himself out in a jet-black shirt and vest, with not so much as a white collar to redeem him; besides having all of four almost white patches on the back of his coat! But don't berate him — who knows but this unique coloring is due to a process unrecognized by the Parisian Worth, but designated by Mr. Darwin as " adaptation "? Most field birds are protected by sparrowy backs, and with his black back, the tendency certainly seems to be to lessen the striking effect with lighter colors, leaving the breast, which is unseen when he is on the grass, as black as may be. In the fall when flying into dangers that necessitate an inconspicuous suit, the bobolink makes amends for the confusion caused in the spring, by adopting the uniform ochraceous tints of his wife. In this dress he joins large companies of his brothers and flies south, where he is known first as the " reedbird," and then, in the rice-fields, as the "ricebird."

What could resemble the old time "needle in the hay-stack" more than a bobolink's nest in a meadow full of high grass? But, do you say, the birds act as a magnet to discover it? That seems to remove all difficulties. But suppose your magnet were bound to make you believe north, south, and east, west? When the bobolinks assure you their nest is — anywhere except where it is — within a radius of five or six rods, you — well, try it some warm day next summer! Here is a bit of my experience.

One day in June I think I have surely found a bobolink's nest. Everything is simplified. Instead of a dozen pairs of birds flying up helter skelter from all parts of the field, there is only one pair, and they kindly give me a line across the meadow ending with a small elm on the west, and a fence on the east. As they only occasionally diverge to an evergreen on the north or go for a run to a distant field on the south, I am confident. In imagination I am already examining the brownish white, deeply speckled eggs and noting the details of the nest. But the best way is to keep perfectly still and let the birds show me just where the nest is, though of course it is only a matter of a few minutes more or less. I sit down in the grass, pull the timothy stems over my dress, make myself look as much as possible like a meadow, and keep one eye on the bobolinks, while appearing to be absorbed with an object on the other side. But they are better actors than I.

Twitter-itter-itter the anxious mother reiterates in a high key as she hovers suggestively over a tuft of grass a few rods away. So soon! My impatience can hardly be restrained. But — the father is coming.

Lingkum-lingkum-lingkum, he vociferates loudly, hovering over a bunch of weeds in just the opposite direction. By this time the mother is atilt of another timothy stem in a new place, looking as if just ready to fly down to her nest. And so they keep it up. I examine all the weeds and tussocks of grass they point out. On nearing one of them, the mother flies about my head with a show of the greatest alarm; my hopes reach certainty — there is nothing there! I look under every nodding buttercup and spreading daisy for yards around only to see Mrs. Robert of Lincoln hovering above a spot she had avoided before. The next day I offer a reward to two children if they will find the nest, but the birds probably practice the same wiles on them — they can discover nothing. What a pity the poor birds can't tell friends from enemies. They treat me as if I were a brigand; but if they knew I wanted to peep at their pretty eggs and admire their housekeeping arrangements, how gladly they would show me about!

After noticing the clear cut, direct flight of the robin, the undulating flight of the bluebird, and the circling and zigzagging of the swift, you will study with interest the labored sallies and eccentricities of the bobolink. When he soars, he turns his wings down till he looks like an open umbrella; and when getting ready to light in the grass puts them up sail fashion, so that the umbrella seems to be turned inside out. Indeed, from the skillful way he uses his wings and tail to steer and balance himself, you might think he had been trained for an acrobat.

The most animated song of the bobolink is given on the wing, although he sings constantly in the grass, and on low trees and bushes. The most exuberantly happy of all our birds, he seems to contain the essence of summer joy and sunshine. " *Bobolinkum-linkum-deah-deah-deah* " he warbles away, the notes fairly tumbling over each other as they pour out of his throat. Up from the midst of the buttercups and daisies he starts and flies along a little way, singing this joyous song with such light-hearted fervor that he is glad to sink down on the stem of some sturdy young timothy before giving his last burst of song.

Thoreau gives the best description I have ever seen of the first notes of the bobolink's song. He says : " I hear the note of a bobolink concealed in the top of an apple-tree behind me. . . . He is just touching the strings of his theorbo, his glassichord, his water organ, and one or two notes globe themselves and fall in liquid bubbles from his tuning throat. It is as if he touched his harp within a vase of liquid melody, and when he lifted it out the notes fell like bubbles from the trembling strings. Methinks they are the most liquidly sweet and melodious sounds I ever heard."

Almost every one gives a different rendering of the bobolink's meaning. The little German children playing in our meadows cry after him in merry mimicry, "*Oncle-dey dunkel-dey oncle-dey dunkel-dey.*" The farm boy calls him the "corn-planting bird," and thinks he says, " *Dig a hole, dig a hole, put it in, put it in, cover 't up, cover 't up, stamp on 't, stamp on 't, step along.*"

VIII.

RUFFED GROUSE ; PARTRIDGE.

THE partridge, or ruffed grouse as he is more properly called, is our first true woods bird. His

colors are the colors of the brown leaves that lie
on the ground, and as he crouches close to the
earth it is no easy task to discover him. The one
thought of the poor persecuted bird seems to be
to keep out of reach of his enemies.

Here, one of his favorite covers is in a quiet
spot where I go to gather ferns — a grove that
" fronts the rising sun " and is full of dappled
maple saplings interspersed with the white birches
that gleam in the morning light and keep birch-
bark scrolls rolled up along their sides ready for
the birds to carry away for their nests. At the
foot of the trees, and close to the moss-covered
drumming-log, ferns stand in pretty groups of all
growths from the tiny green sprays and the soft
uncurling downy balls to the full grown arching
fronds whose backs are dotted with brown fruit;
while, as a protecting hedge along the front of the
grove, great masses of the tender green mountain
fern give their delicate fragrance to the air. But
pass by this hiding place, and a sudden *whirr*
through the bushes, first from one startled bird
and then another, tells you they have flown before
you. Approach the drumming-log when the air
has been resounding with exultant blows — the
noise stops, not a bird is to be seen.

As we feed the partridges in our woods and
never allow any hunting there, in winter the birds
venture about the house for food. The Norway
spruces by the garden afford a warm shelter, and

there, under the boughs, corn is kept for them on barrels and boxes. On the other side of the house, in front of the dining-room window, is a similar store for the blue jays and gray squirrels; and as they sometimes visit the partridges' table, the latter often fly around the house to see if the squirrels' corn tastes any better than theirs.

The first snowy morning they appear we have to peek through the shutters very cautiously, for they are painfully shy, crouching in the snow, listening tremulously to the least sound from the house, looking about every time they pick up a kernel of corn, and whirring off back to their evergreens if a window or blind chances to be thrown open. But they soon lose their fears, and some mornings we find their pretty footprints in the snow on the piazza.

One winter they seemed to show a fondness for music, often coming close to the house as I was playing the piano. Indeed they and the squirrels must both have followed the Pied Piper of Hamelin — the squirrels not only nibble their corn with complacent satisfaction when the music box is wound for them, but have even let themselves be stroked when a peculiarly pathetic air was whistled! Who dare say what forest concerts the pretty creatures may get up on the long winter evenings when they are tired frolicking on the moonlit snow!

Still the partridges seem to like the bright red

berries of the cranberry-tree even better than they do music, and we have been much amused watching their attempts to get the berries from a bush by the garden. Sometimes they stand in the snow underneath and jump for them ; but one day when the bush was covered with ice one adventurous bird flew up on a branch and nearly turned a somersault in trying to lean over and pick off the berries and at the same time keep hold of the slippery perch.

But our chief pleasure is in watching the partridges from the bay window of the dining-room. The young men are as proud as turkey-cocks of the handsome black ruffs for which they were dubbed " ruffed grouse," and when they strut before the ladies, raising their crests, erecting their spread tails, and puffing out the ruffs over their shoulders they remind one forcibly of the lordly cock. In matter of fact they do belong to the same family, — that of the gallinaceous birds, — and many of their mannerisms betray the relationship. Their way of scratching in the snow, resting their weight on one foot and scratching with the other, is like that of the common hen, and their drumming is the finished performance that is caricatured by Chanticleer. Drumming with the partridge is a joy. He beats the air with his wings till it must needs sing for him, and the music is full of refreshing pictures of green mossy logs, arching ferns, and the cool shade of the woods.

IX.

RUBY-THROATED HUMMING-BIRD.

Did you ever see a humming-bird sitting on a
bare branch of a towering tree? Until you have
you will scarcely appreciate what a wee mite of a
bird it is. Indeed I find it hard to think of it
as a bird at all. It seems more like a fairy, " a
glittering fragment of a rainbow," as Audubon
calls it, or as some one else has said, —

> " Like a gem or a blossom on pinions,"

something too dainty and airy to have even three
inches of actual length. It seems like the winged
spirit of color as it comes humming through the
air to hover over the flowers on the piazza, its
body like green beryl, and its throat glancing fire.
Like Puck it might boast that it could " put a
girdle round about the earth in forty minutes,"
for while we are wondering at its friendliness it
darts off and is gone like the flash of a diamond.

In this vicinity the garden of Mrs. Bagg seems
to be one of the favorite haunts of the humming-
birds, and she has kindly given me some notes on
her experiences with them. She says : —

" In confinement they do not appear to pine for
freedom, beating themselves against the wires like
other birds, but seem contented and at home from
the first. I kept a pair caged a whole summer,

feeding them with water sweetened with honey or
sugar. When I put a cup of their food in the
cage they would alight on my fingers, and with
their long flexible tongue suck off the honey I had
accidentally spilled. In disposition they are too
pugnacious to live as harmoniously as one would
expect or desire, sometimes pursuing one another
around the cage with great ferocity, and such in-
conceivable rapidity that their tiny forms seemed
resolved into absolute *sound*. I frequently permitted them to fly about the room for exercise,
but they never returned voluntarily to their cage.
When caught they did not resist and struggle,
but saw the door of their prison-house closed upon
them without a complaint. They had never a sick
or unhappy day through the whole summer, but
when the cold days of autumn approached they
began to droop, although their cage was hung in
the warmest place in the room. For three days
they hung suspended to their perches by their
feet, and did not relax the hold while life lasted.
I have found them clinging to vines and shrubbery in that manner on cold mornings after a
frost, but though seemingly lifeless the warmth of
the hand would revive them.

"Some years a few are unaccountably tardy
about migrating; at other times they make the
mistake of coming too early in spring. Undoubt-
edly most of them migrate in August, but with
them, as in every other community, there are al-

ways some laggards as well as bold pioneers. I
once found one in my house on a very cold morning in the fall. He was probably sleeping on some
house-plants that had been brought in from the
frost the previous night, and was too benumbed
with cold to know it. I caught and fed him, as it
would have been barbarous to turn him out in the
cold. He soon became a great pet, and was tame
as a kitten.

"One day two gentlemen entered the room
where his cage was hanging, both wearing tall
hats. He fell immediately to the bottom of the
cage, with wings outspread, eyes closed, body rigid,
and with every appearance of death. We took
him in our hands and warmed him by the fire.
He still remained motionless. We decided that
those *hats* had frightened him to death. With a
heavy heart I laid him aside, intending to embalm
him at my leisure.

"A few minutes later my friends left the house.
Directly after the door closed I heard a humming
and buzzing in the room. Looking up, there was
my bird circling around the room in the most hila-
rious manner. Who can tell whether his apparent
death was not counterfeited? If it was not feigned,
why did he revive the moment the door was closed
and I was alone?

"If you capture one out of doors and hold
him in your hand he will practice the same
ruse, stretching himself out, stiff and motionless.

Thrown off your guard you stoop to examine your prize, when lo! your hand is empty and your bird nearly out of sight before you have time to recover from the astonishment.

"Towards the humble-bee he manifests the utmost ill-will, a veritable 'dog in the manger' spirit, driving him away from one flower after another till the bee in pure desperation turns on his persecutor. There are surely sweets enough for all, and he knows it. Still it may be possible that his animosity is aroused more by a personal aversion he has to the bee than by more selfish considerations. We will give him the benefit of the doubt. He is fond of silence, and will often sit half an hour together on a dead twig wrapt in the profoundest meditation, and doubtless the incessant droning of the bees disturbs his reflections and irritates him beyond endurance. I had once in my garden a ribbon-bed of white and rose colored Lamium. In its unsullied beauty it was like a dream of poetry. Every flower was perfect with an unsurpassed and delicate loveliness. One sunny morning I observed an unusual number of humming-birds and bees working among the blossoms. Presently there was a commotion! The humming-birds had united to drive the bees away, darting at them furiously, uttering at the same time their spiteful, piping cries. The bees, intent on seeking their breakfast, at first gave up good-naturedly and flew to some other flower, only to

be driven from that a moment later. At length
forbearance ceased to be a virtue, and the temper
of the apathetic bee was aroused. A fierce battle
ensued. They pursued one another around and
around that flower bed, over and under and
through the flowers, sometimes the birds and then
the bees having the vantage. Their rage knew no
bounds, and they fought till sheer exhaustion com-
pelled them to desist. Every flower was torn to
shreds, not a whole blossom remaining."

The nest of the humming-bird is as delicate as
the little creature itself. It is built in the form
of a small cup, saddled upon a horizontal limb,
and covered on the outside with lichens which
make it look like a knob on the branch. The
child who discovers a humming-bird's nest is cred-
ited with sharp eyes.

X.

MEADOW-LARK.

To many, the meadow-lark is only a voice, but
if you follow the rule laid down at the beginning
of your work, and are determined to see as well
as hear, you will have little trouble in finding the
owner of the plaintive call that rises so mysteriously out of the grass.

Focus your glass on the meadow, and listen
carefully for the direction of the sound. As the

lark is very much the color of the dead grass that covers the ground when he first comes north, and of the dry stubble left after the summer mowing, he is somewhat hard to see. When you have found him, it is a delightful surprise to see that

the brownish yellow disguise of his back is relieved, not, indeed, by a sable robe like the bobolink's, but by a throat of brilliant yellow, set off by a large black crescent.

The meadow-lark has two notable characteristics. Belonging to the blackbird family, he is a walker, and when he flies you will see that he is also one of the few birds marked by prominent white outer tail feathers. The peculiarities of his labored flight are exactly described by Shelley when he says, in his Ode to the Skylark, "Thou dost *float* and *run*." Flying seems hard work for him, and he does as little of it as possible. When he starts up from the meadow, he goes in a direct line to the tree he wishes to reach. Like the bobolink, he nests in fields and lays his eggs in a coil of dried grass on the ground.

In variety and execution the famous song of the European lark may be superior to that of our own Eastern lark, though Wilson holds that ours excels it in "sweetness of voice." The mournful melody of the meadow-lark is full of poetic suggestions; he is the hermit thrush of the meadows, and where the light-hearted bobolink's song jostles the sunbeams, he is as solitary and pensive as the lonely hermit when it thrills the hush of the sunset after-glow with its fervid Te Deum.

XI.

BLACK-CAPPED CHICKADEE; TITMOUSE.

READ Emerson's "Titmouse" and you will recognize this charming little bird without the aid of your glass. Not only in spring and fall, but in the coldest winter days you will hear what Thoreau calls the "silver tinkling" *chick-a-dee-dee-dee-dee*, *chick-a-dee-dee-dee-dee* ringing through the air. When you hear it, if you look carefully over the trees you will see a fluffy little body dressed out in a black hood whose sombre tone is relieved by whitish side pieces, a vest to match the sides of the hood, and a dark gray coat for contrast. Clinging to the side of a tree one minute, and hanging upside down pecking at the moss on a branch the next, it is flitting about hither and thither so busily that unless you draw near you will hardly catch a glimpse of its black cap and gray and white clothes. You need not fear scaring it, for it has the most winning confidence in man, inspecting the trees in the front yard or those in the woods with the same trustful unconcern.

You are inclined to think that the busy chickadee takes no time to meditate, and sees only the bright side of life ; and when you hear its plaintive minor whistle piercing the woods, you wonder if it can have come from the same little creature whose merry *chick-a-dee-dee* you know so well. Thoreau calls this plaintive whistle the spring phœbe's note of the chickadee, and gives its winter call as *day*, *day*, *day*. When happy, the chickadee is the best company one could hope for on a winter's walk ; when busy it seems to realize perpetual motion ; and when it gives up its ordinary pursuits and prepares to rear a family, it goes to work in the same whole-souled fashion. Leaving civilization with its many distractions, it goes into the woods, and that is the last you see or hear of it until fall. Even there it is not content to sit perched up on top of an open nest, but builds in the side of a stump or a dead stub, and retires from the world with the determination of a nun.

You will wonder at first how such a tiny bill as the chickadee's can be used as a pickaxe, but if you notice it carefully you will see that, without being clumsy, it is very stout, for it is arched enough to give it strength. Of course the chickadee sometimes nests in natural cavities in trees ; and Audubon says old woodpeckers' holes are occasionally used; but most writers agree in thinking that it usually makes its own excavation, occasionally in comparatively hard wood.

One morning I was hurrying noisily through the underbrush of a clearing to get home in time for breakfast, when, suddenly, I came face to face with a pair of chickadees. Even then they did not stir, but sat eying me calmly for several seconds. I suspected a nest, and when they had flown off, I discovered the opening in a decayed stub close by my side. The stub was a small one, being perhaps eight or ten inches in diameter and four and a half feet high. The entrance was about a foot from the top, and the nest itself a foot or more below this. What a tasteful little structure it was ! Although out of sight, it was far prettier than most bird-houses on exhibition in the forest. Bits of fresh green moss gave it a dainty air, and brought out the dark gray of the squirrel or rabbit fur that made it snug and warm. I was tempted to wonder where the fur came from — had this innocent chickadee tweaked it out of the back of some preoccupied animal? Perhaps the demure little recluse has a spice of wickedness after all, and its satisfaction in its secure retreat has something of exultant mischief in it!

In any case, it sometimes takes unfair advantage, for this fall I saw a chickadee deliberately lying in wait for his breakfast, just as a spider would. I was passing a Norway spruce when I caught sight of him pecking away on the under side of one of the lower branches. Soon he pulled out a large white chrysalis-like ball, flew up on a branch and sat there till he disposed of it. Then he went back and hung himself, upside down, to the branch, just below the place where the first morsel had come from. Balder, my big Newfoundland, and I were within five feet of the little rogue, but he did not care for that. There he clung for as much as two or three minutes, perfectly motionless except when he turned his head to give us a preoccupied look. Then suddenly he picked down and drew out a small white worm, and flew up into the branch with a triumphant little cry, as much as to say, " Ha, ha, I got you after all! "

XII.

CUCKOO; RAIN CROW.

UNLESS you follow the cuckoo to his haunts, you rarely see him. Now and then, perhaps, you catch a glimpse of his long brown body as he comes silently out of an orchard, an overgrown garden, or a clump of bushes, to disappear swiftly in a heavily leaved tree or mass of shrubbery where he suspects a fresh supply of insects.

A third longer than the robin, the cuckoo is a slender, olive-brown bird with a light breast. The two species are very similar in appearance and

habit, but in the yellow-billed there are distinct white spots known as "thumb marks" on the under side of the tail. The black-billed cuckoo is a plainer bird, its only striking peculiarity being its bright red eyelids.

You will do well to remember the rhythm of the cuckoo's notes. It may save you an experience I had one fall. I supposed the birds had left for the South, but hearing a regular *kuk-kuk-kuk* coming from the woods, and being especially anxious to study the cuckoo's habits, I left the raspberry patch where I was watching for rare warblers, and hurried off in search of the wandering voice. What a treat! — to be able to see a cuckoo after all! I crept along with scrupulous care, begrudging the time my caution cost me, but determined not to lose this last chance. What if he should fly off before I could get there! But no — I began to exult — *kuk-kuk-kuk* came loud and clear as I stopped to listen for the direction of the sound. I must be almost up to him. Oh, that I could sweep all the noisy dead leaves into the ditch! I look about anxiously for moss and old logs to step on. There! Grasping my note-book in one hand, with the other I raise my glass. A mischievous looking chipmunk, sitting erect on top of a mossy stump, suddenly jumps off into the leaves and — the sound stops!

XIII.

YELLOW HAMMER ; FLICKER.

W HEN people attempt to give their children
descriptive names they generally meet with the
success of the colored woman who christened her
little girl " Lillie White " only to see her grow
to be the darkest of her ebony family.   But local
bird names are more like nicknames ; they usually
touch facts, not hopes, and hint the most striking
features of coloring, song, flight, and habit.   As
you have discovered, this is true of the bluebird,
chimney swift, catbird, keel-tailed blackbird, humming - bird, and meadow - lark ; and looking over
the yellow hammer's thirty-six common names
given by Mr. Colburn in the Audubon Magazine
for June, 1887, you will get a fair description of
the bird.   As he flies over your head in the field
your first impression is of a large yellow bird —
he is of the size of the crow blackbird — and
on the list you find " yellow hammer," " yellow
jay," and " pique-bois jaune " ; but as the yellow
light comes mainly from his bright yellow shafts
and the gold of the underside of his wings
and tail, you have also " yellow-shafted woodpecker," and " golden-winged woodpecker."   His
dark back and the large white spot at the base of
his tail, though conspicuous in flight, are not dignified by a name ; but when he lights on the side

of a tree or an old stub you recognize him as a
" woodpecker." With the help of your glass you
also see the bright red crescent on the back of his
head, for which he is probably called " crescent
bird." There he clings, fastening his claws firmly
in the bark, and bracing himself with the stiff
quills of his tail, so that his convexity of outline
almost amounts to a half circle as he bends forward to " hammer " on the wood. This is the
best time to use your glass, for he is quite a shy
bird, and except when engaged in his favorite
work, is hard to observe satisfactorily, even at a
respectful distance. His dark back proves to be
barred with black, and following him as he circles
up the tree you get a glimpse of his breast that
discloses a large black collar separating his thickly
spotted breast from the plain light throat.

The song of the yellow hammer is like the German *th* — he has n't any. He has a variety of cries
and calls, however, and a trill that sounds like a
great rattle shaken in the air. Mr. Colburn at-
tributes twelve of his names to imitations of these
various sounds; clape, cave-duc, fiddler, flicker,
hittock, hick-wall, ome-tuc, piute or peerit, wake-
up, yaffle, yarrup, and yucker.

Mr. Ingersoll refers " flicker " to his flight, and
if you watch your yellow hammer till he flies off
to another tree you will see that the adjective describes his peculiar but characteristic woodpecker
flight better than the most labored description.

Mr. Colburn says he is called "taping bird" from it, because he looks as if "measuring off tape."

If you are persevering enough to follow him to his nest — and you never feel thoroughly acquainted with birds any more than with people

until you see them in their homes — you will discover why he is called "high-hold," "high-holder," and "high-hole" — that is, if the nest he has made is one of the high ones. Sometimes yellow hammers build very low. However this may be, the entrance to the nest is a large round hole, cut out of the wood of the tree, as the pile of chips on the ground attests. Inside, the hole is very deep and the white eggs are laid on the chips at the bottom. The usual number of eggs is six.

A gentleman tells me a curious case of miscalculation on the part of a yellow hammer that built in an old apple-tree near his house. He says the old birds kept bringing food to the nest so long that he thought something must be wrong, and went to investigate. The nest was just within his reach, and he found that, as he had supposed, the birds were more than large enough to fly. In fact they were so large they could not get out of the mouth of the nest, and were actually imprisoned there! The gentleman got an axe and cut out the opening for them, and the next morning the brood had flown.

Knowing the habits of the yellow hammer, you wonder why there is no name to credit him with the work he does for us in eating the boring ants that eviscerate our noblest trees ; and you are still more surprised to find no name to stamp him a field and ground woodpecker, because his devotion to ant-hills and other ground preserves is one of the characteristics that distinguish him from the other woodpeckers. Possibly the name "woodpecker lark" may refer to his custom of hunting in the fields.

XIV.

BALTIMORE ORIOLE; FIRE-BIRD; GOLDEN ROBIN; HANG-NEST.

WILSON notices the interesting fact that our oriole was named by Linnæus in honor of Lord Baltimore, whose colors were black and orange.

He is shorter than the robin, and compared with that plump alderman is slenderly and delicately built — much more in the form of the blackbirds. His back is black instead of grayish-brown, and his breast orange instead of dull reddish. In habit, he contrasts still more strongly with the robin. Who ever saw Sir Baltimore watching for fish-worms in the grass, or taking possession of a crotch in the piazza? — and, on the other hand, who ever saw a robin hold his dinner under his claw and peck it to pieces as the orioles and their cousins the blackbirds do? The oriole is comparatively shy, and has a nervous, excitable temperament, while the robin is not only social but phlegmatic. Then the call of the fire-bird is shriller, and pitched on a higher key; while his love song is an elaborate poem in melody, compared with the blunt courtship of robin redbreast — just watch this graceful suitor some morning as he bows and scrapes before his lady-love to the rhythm of his exquisitely modulated song. Now running high and loud with joyful exultant love, then curving into a low, soft cadence, vibrating with caressing tenderness, it finally rounds off with broken notes of entreaty so full of courtly devotion and submission, yet, withal, so musical and earnest with tender love, that you feel sure his suit can never be denied.

When the oriole comes to build his nest and you compare his work with that of the robin, you feel that you have an artistic Queen Anne beside a rude mud hovel. The term hang-nest is strictly applicable. The birds are skillful weavers and build long, delicate, pocket-shaped nests that look as if made of gray moss. These they hang from the end of a branch, as if thinking of the first line of the old nursery rhyme, —

> " When the wind blows the cradle will rock,
> When the bough breaks the cradle will fall," —

and, indeed, the cradles are built by such clever workmen that the bough must needs break to give them a fall. The nest looks as if it barely touched the twigs from which it hangs, but when you examine it you may find that the gray fibres have woven the wood in so securely that the nest would have to be torn in pieces before it could be loosened from the twigs. What is the nest made of? It shines as if woven with threads of gray silk, but it must be field silk from the stems of plants. And the horse hairs? Mr. Burroughs tells of one oriole who went bravely into the back part of a horse stable for its hair lining. Sometimes a bit of twine or gay worsted thrown on the grass is gladly accepted, and Nuttall once saw an oriole carry off a piece of lampwick ten or twelve feet long.

In Northampton I witnessed an interesting case which proved that skill in nest making as well as other crafts comes by hard-earned experience, and, consequently, that manual training should be introduced into all bird schools! A pair of young and inexperienced orioles fell in love and set out, with the assurance of most brides and grooms, to build a home for themselves. They succeeded admirably in the selection of their building site, but then the trouble began. The premise that all young lovers are weavers or architects sometimes leads to dire syllogistic conclusions. Was it the pressing business of the honeymoon that interfered with the weaving, or was it because this young couple had not yet learned how to pull together that their threads got in a snarl and their gray pocket was all awry? Whatever the reason, the cradle was altogether too short to rock well, and was skewed up in such a fashion that some of the baby birds would have been sure of a smothering. Like Grimm's clever Elsie the birds foresaw all these dangers, and actually left the completed nest to be tossed by the wind while they went off to try again in another place. It is believed to be unusual for two young birds to pair together.

XV.

BARN SWALLOW.

THE barn swallow is the handsomest and best known of the swallows. It is lustrous steel blue above, and has a partial collar of the same between the deep chocolate of the chin and throat and the pale chestnut of the breast.

What a contrast to the ugly so-called " chimney swallow " ! And not in coloring only. Compare its long forked tail with the short, square, bristly tail of the swift. And then watch its flight — the coursing of a Pegasus beside the trotting of a racer ! The swift has wonderful wing power, but no grace. It flies as if under wager, and when hunting, its path might be marked off by angles, for it zigzags like a bat. But the barn swallow's course is all curves. It has the freest flight of any bird I have ever seen. It seems absolutely without effort or constraint.

The swallows are so agile they often dart down as you drive along the road, and circle around and around you, managing dexterously to keep just ahead of the horses. At other times they run and circle away over the fields and through the sky, and at sunset often haunt our rivers or lakes, skimming low over the surface and sometimes dipping down for a drink as they go.

At rest, they sit side by side on the ridge-pole

of a barn or on a telegraph wire, where they look
like rows of little mutes.   It is funny enough to
see them light on a wire.   Fluttering over it for
a moment before settling down, they sway back
and forth till you are sure they must fall off.

The roads afford them much occupation.   When
not making statistics about the passers-by, or col-
lecting mud for their nests, they take dust baths
in the road.   They usually build inside barns or
covered bridges, lining their nests with feathers,
but a case is recorded of a nest under the eaves of
a house, which was made entirely of " rootlets and
grass," though thickly lined with downy chicken
feathers.   Mr. Burroughs tells of a barn nest
" saddled in the loop of a rope that was pendant
from a peg in the peak."

Of the notes of the barn swallow Mr. Bicknell
says : " An almost universal misconception re-
gards the swallows as a tribe of songless birds.
But the barn swallow has as true claims to song
as many species of long-established recognition as
song birds. Its song is a low, chattering trill . . .
often terminating with a clear liquid note with an
accent as of interrogation, not unlike one of the
notes of the canary. This song is wholly distinct
from the quick, double-syllabled note which so
constantly escapes the bird during flight."

XVI.

BELTED KINGFISHER.

THE robin lives on neighborly terms in our
dooryard, the swift secretes himself in our chimneys, the humming-bird hovers in our gardens,
the barn swallow circles around our barns, the
catbird talks to himself in our orchards, the oriole
hangs his " hammock " from our elms, the bobolink holds gay possession of our fields till the
mower comes to dispute his claim, and the yellow
hammer appoints himself inspector general of our
ant-hills, fence-posts, and tree trunks ; but the
kingfisher cares nothing for us or our habitations.
He goes off by himself into the heart of the wilderness, not to crouch among the brown leaves on
the ground like the partridge, but to fly high and

far over river and lake, calling loudly to the echoes as he goes.

He is the most marked of the trillers, having a loud, rapid call that Wilson compares to a watchman's rattle, and that, as Mr. Burroughs ingen-

iously suggests, reminds you of an alarm clock. He usually gives it when on the wing, and if on hearing him you look up in time, you will see a large, ungainly slate-blue bird, with an odd flight — his short tail making him out of proportion so that his wings seem too far back. As he flies over, you note his big, heavily-crested head, his dark collar, and his glistening white throat. If he lights on a dead stub by the water, and you can see the compact, oily plumage that is adapted for cold plunges, you will think him handsome in spite of his topheaviness. He sits like the catbird, and watches the fish come toward the surface. But before they know what has happened they are wriggling in his bill. After catching a fish he quickly carries it back to his perch, to be devoured at his leisure.

The kingfisher shows us a new style of nest, though it might seem that there had been variety enough before. There was the " adobe house " of the robin, the coarse bundle of sticks gathered by the crow, the exquisite lichen-covered cup of the humming-bird, the loose, clumsy-looking nests of the catbird and cuckoo, the frame house rented by the bluebird, the tiny wall pocket glued to the chimney by the swift, the grass houses of the bob-olink and meadow-lark, the mud bowl of the barn swallow, the airy gray pocket of the oriole, and the snug wooden retreats of the chickadee and yellow hammer. But here is something stranger than any of them — a burrow in the earth, that might well be the hole of some shy animal rather than the home of a bird. It is usually dug in the banks of rivers or streams.

As the kingfisher spends most of his time on the wing, his feet are small and weak, different enough from the powerful feet and claws of the

blackbirds and orioles. What a woodsman the
kingfisher must be! Do the hemlock's longest
branches tip to the east? Does the lichen grow
on the north side of the trees? Ask him for his
compass. He needs no trail. Follow him and he
will teach you the secrets of the forest. For here
lies the witchcraft of our new world halcyon,
rather than in the charming of sailors' lives, or in
the stilling of the sea.

XVII.

CHIP-BIRD OR CHIPPY; HAIR-BIRD; CHIPPING SPARROW; SOCIAL SPARROW.

WE have already had "chimney swallows" that
were not swallows, crow blackbirds that were not
crows, partridges that were grouse, and kingfishers
that dug holes in the ground, besides bluebirds
and humming-birds and robins and chickadees and
catbirds and cuckoos, all crowded together; and
now we are coming to that vexatious family, the
sparrows. How can any one be expected to remember such a medley long enough to know the
birds out of doors? I never really knew them
until I pigeon-holed them, and I believe that is
the best way. But how shall we go to work?

Ornithologists separate our birds into seventeen
orders, and divide these into numerous families
and genera and species. We should have to turn

pension-office clerks to get pigeon-holes enough for them! But twelve of the seventeen we shall leave entirely alone, — the divers, all kinds of swimmers, waders, herons, cranes, parrots, and others that most of us never see outside of museums. Of the five orders left, four are quickly disposed of. The partridge will be our only representative of the "gallinaceous birds," the cuckoos and king-fishers of the order of "cuckoos, etc.," the wood-peckers of the "woodpeckers, etc.," and the swift, humming-bird, night-hawk, and whippoorwill of the "goatsuckers, swifts, etc."

There are so few of these, and they are so scattered, that it does not seem worth while to give up part of our pigeon-holes to them, so we will put them away in a drawer by themselves, and keep our pigeon-holes free for the one order left, — the highest of all, — that of the "perching birds." It has twenty-one families, but we need only fourteen holes because there are seven families that we shall not take up. So our best way is to paste the label "perching birds" over our fourteen holes, and then, while remembering that we have left out seven families, number each hole and put in the birds as they come in their natural order of development from low to high.

The crow goes in No. 2 by himself at present. The bobolink, meadow-lark, crow blackbird, and oriole all go into No. 3, because they belong to the family of "blackbirds, orioles, etc.," although they represent different branches, or genera. Chippy goes into No. 4 to wait for the other "finches, sparrows, etc.," the barn swallow will go into No. 6, which belongs to "the swallows," the catbird into No. 10, the chickadee into No. 12, and the robin and bluebird into No. 14, — the last hole, — as they belong to the most highly developed family of all the birds, that of the "thrushes, bluebirds, etc."

This simplifies matters. The chimney swift belongs to an entirely different order from the swallows, — a much lower one, — and so was put in the drawer, together with the kingfisher, whose feet are weak and who nests in the ground. Now all the "perching birds" we have had fall readily into place. The crow is by himself in No. 2, as the blackbirds in No. 3 differ from him in having wives smaller than themselves, and in anatomical and technical peculiarities that are the foundation of all the divisions we have.

But here is chippy in No. 4; let us see how he is related to the other birds. First, what does he look like? Although one of those "little gray birds" that vex the spirit of the tyro, he is well known as the smallest and most friendly of our sparrows. All the sparrows are small, dull colored birds, none of them being much more than half as large as a robin. But he is marked by a reddish-brown cap, edged by a delicate white line over eye and cheek. His back is streaked with grayish-

brown and black, his wings are crossed by narrow
whitish bars, and underneath he is a pure light
ash color.

Notice the bill chippy has to crack seeds with.
It is the short, thick, conical bill of the family,
and contrasts not only with the long slender bills
of the worm-eating robin and bluebird in No.
14, but with those of the oriole, crow blackbird,
and meadow-lark in No. 3. The bobolink shows
the nearness of No. 3 and 4 in his partly conical
bill, and also in flight, though, by coloring, he is
more closely related to the crow in No. 2. It is
hardly necessary to suggest the differences that
separate chippy from the chimney swift, the ruffed
grouse, the humming-bird, the cuckoo, and the
ant-eating yellow hammer.

Of our common sparrows chippy alone has no
real song, but he trills away monotonously, —
by the hour, you are tempted to think, — with
cheerful perseverance that would grace a better
cause. He is called "hair-bird" because he lines
his nest with horse or cow hair, and when you
think of the close observation and industry it takes
to find this hair you will recognize not only the
power of inherited habit but the fitness of the
name *hair-bird*.

Last summer a chipping sparrow built in a jas-
mine bush in the crotch of a neighbor's piazza.
When the little mother was startled by intruders
she would dart into the bush, crouch down, flatten

her head, and try to make herself invisible, but
she had too many frights and at last abandoned
her nest.   In a grape-vine on top of a trellis in
the garden in front of the cottage another chippy
had built.   She seemed to be fearless, never stirring even when we stood at the foot of the trellis
and stared at her.

I found several nests in Norway spruces.   One
was near a farm-house.   It was on a bough hidden
so skillfully under an evergreen twig that I had
much ado to find it, and there was barely room for
even the small mother bird to get up to it.   But the
four little dark blue eggs wreathed with purplish
dots around the larger ends, as they lay clustered
on their mat of brown rootlets, made a sight to
repay a longer hunt.   With all her care the poor
mother was not able to conceal her little ones.   A
hungry chipmunk discovered them, and was shot
by the farmer when it was swallowing the last one
of the four.

In summer the chipping birds haunt the piazza,
coming almost to our feet for crumbs.   Last season
two broods were brought by their mothers, and it
was diverting to watch them.   The mothers drove
each other about in a scandalous fashion, and, what
was worse, would not feed each other's children,
but turned their backs in the most hard-hearted
way even when the hungry youngsters ran up in
front of them and stood with wide open bills teasing for food.   As the babies grew older I suspect

their mothers poisoned their minds, too, for as nearly as I could make out a coldness grew up between the families of infants.

The old chipping birds are very intelligent. The turn of the head and the quick glance from the eye show that their familiar bravery is due to no thoughtless confidence, but is based on keen observation and bird wit.

The young birds seem more trustful and are dear fluffy little creatures. When they get to be as big as their mothers and know perfectly well how to feed themselves, the lazy babies will often stand helplessly right in the middle of a handful of crumbs, and chirr at their mother till she picks the crumbs up and drops them in their bills.

One day I found a young chippy sitting on the picket of a fence. His mother soon flew up onto the picket next to him with his dinner in her bill and leaned over trying to reach it across. It was a comical proceeding, the baby fluttering his wings, opening his mouth, crying out and bobbing toward his mother while she stretched across till — well, both birds came near a tumble before they gave it up.

Chipping birds are always about, in the garden, on the lawn, and around the house. The back door with its boundless possibilities in the crumb line attracts them strongly. At one house, for several years, a number of them came to the back yard every day when the chickens were fed. They sat on the fence till the first rush and scramble were over, and then flew down among the hens to get their dinner.

XVIII.

THE song sparrow, of course, goes into the same pigeon-hole as chippy — No. 4, " finches, sparrows, etc.," — showing the same sparrow traits in coloring, size, bill, and flight; and the same contrasts with the crow in No. 2, the " blackbirds, orioles, etc.," in No. 3, the " swallows " in No. 6, and the robin and bluebird among the "thrushes, bluebirds, etc.," of No. 14. But with all this, our little friend has a marked individuality, and differs from his small cousin chippy in temper and charm. I may be prejudiced, but while I admire chippy for his bravery and intelligence I do not find him as winsome as this simple little bird with his homely cheeriness.

In the spring the song sparrow comes North a few days after the robin, and although the chill from the snow banks gives him a sore throat that makes his voice husky, you may hear him singing as brightly as if he had come back on purpose to bring spring to the poor snow-bound farmers. Even his chirp — of rich contralto quality compared with the thin chip of his cousin — has a genuine happy ring that raises one's spirits ; and when he throws up his head and sings the sweet song that gives him his name, you feel sure the world is worth living in.

The song sparrow's brown coat has little beauty, but his dark breastpin, surrounded by brown streaks, sets off his light gray waistcoat to advantage ; and the brown topknot that he raises when interested gives him a winning air of sympathetic attention.

The song sparrows are not about the house as much as the chippies, and last summer they began coming for crumbs a week later in the nesting season than their ubiquitous cousins. Then it was amusing to see the business-like way in which they hopped about, their tails perked up and their wings close to their sides. There was one that walked like a blackbird, and when he ran it seemed a waste of energy — he had so much more to do than if he had hopped !

The usual note of the song sparrow is a rich " *tschip,*" as Thoreau gives it; but when nesting it has an odd thin chip that sounds so like the note of a young bird that it deceived me into hunting through the bushes when the old bird who was really making it was in plain sight. The sparrow's song is the first set song likely to attract your attention when listening to the birds near the house, and as Thoreau says, is " more honest-sounding than most." The song consists of one high note repeated three times, and a rapid run down the scale and back; but it varies greatly with individuals, and almost every writer renders it differently.

In choosing the site for its nest, the song sparrow adapts itself to circumstances with the grace of a true philosopher. At one time content with making a rude mat of straw at the bottom of a roadside brush heap, at another it builds in a willow, using the woolly catkins to soften the bed; and frequently it nests right on the ground, when the farmers call it the " ground sparrow." But the prettiest site of any I have ever known was in a sweetbriar bush on the edge of the garden. Here the little mother could be lulled into her noon-day nap by the droning of the bumble-bees buzzing about the garden; or, if she chose, watch the fluttering butterflies and quivering humming-birds hovering over the bright flowers. Every breath of air brought her the perfume of the briar leaves, and when the pink buds unfolded she could tell off the days of her brooding by the petals that fluttered to the ground.

XIX.

BLUE JAY.

THE blue jay comes with a dash and a flourish. As Thoreau says, he " blows the trumpet of winter." . Unlike the chickadee, whose prevailing tints match the winter sky, and whose gentle *day-day-day* chimes with the softly falling snows, the blue jay would wake the world up. His " clarionet " peals over the villages asleep in the snow-drifts as if it would rouse even the smoke that drowses over their white roofs. He brings the vigor and color of winter. He would send the shivering stay-at-homes jingling merrily over the fields, and start the children coasting down the hills. *Wake-up, wake-up, come-out, come-out* he calls, and blows a blast to show what winter is good for.

And so he flashes about, and screams and scolds till we crawl to the window to look at him. Ha! what a handsome bird! He has found the breakfast hung on the tree for him and clings to it pecking away with the appetite of a Greenlander. Not a hint of winter in his coloring! Note his purplish back as he bends over, the exquisite cobalt blue, touched off with black and white on his wings, and the black barring on the tightly closed tail he is bracing himself by. How distinguished his dark necklace and handsome blue crest make him look! There! he is off again, and before we think where he is going we hear the echo of his rousing *phe-phay*, *phe-phay* from the depths of the woods.

In many places the jays are common winter residents, pitching their tents with the hens and barnyard animals and comporting themselves with familiar assurance. But in this region they are irregular guests. Sometimes they are here for a few days in the fall, or visit us when the hawks return in spring, teasing the young observer by imitating the cry of the redtailed hawk. But if the fancy takes them they spend the winter with us, showing comparatively little of the timidity they feel in some localities.

Last fall a party of jays stayed here for some time, but when I was congratulating myself on having them for the winter, they left, and did not return till the middle of January. Then one morning one of them appeared suddenly on a tree in front of the window. He seemed to have been there before, for he flew straight down to the corn boxes by the dining-room. The gray squirrels had nibbled out the sweetest part of the kernels, and he acted dissatisfied with what was left, dropping several pieces after he had picked them up. But at last he swallowed a few kernels and then took three or four in his bill at once and flew up in a maple. He must have deposited some of them in a crotch at the body of the tree, for after he had broken one in two under his claw — striking it with "sledge-hammer blows" — he went back to the crotch, picked up something, flew back on the branch, and went through the process over again. The second time he flew down to the corn boxes he did the same thing — ate two or three kernels, and then filled his bill full and flew off — this time out of sight. Since then I have often seen him carry his corn off in the same way, giving his head a little toss to throw the kernels back

in his bill as he was loading up. Wilson calls
attention to the fact that by this habit of carrying
off kernels and seeds, the jay becomes an important tree-planting agent.

What a good business man the blue jay would
make! All his motions are like the unique loading up performance — time - saving, decided, direct. Once during the first morning after his return he flew down to the boxes from the tree over
them and came so straight he looked as if falling
through the air. He pecked at the bark of the
trees as indifferently as he had examined the corn
the squirrels had nibbled, but I thought he drank
with some gusto. He seemed to be catching the
rain drops that were running down the sides of
the trees and filling the crevices of the bark.

After he had flown off and the gray squirrels
were comfortably settled at breakfast, he came
dashing back round the corner in such a hurry
he almost struck the squirrel on the lower corn
box. The first thing I saw was a confusion of
blue feathers and gray fur, and then a blue jay
flying off to the evergreen, and a gray squirrel
shaking his tail excitedly and starting from one
side of the box to the other trying to collect his
wits. By this time the blue jay had recovered
from his surprise, and seeing that it was only a
squirrel, hopped about in the spruce as full of
business as if the collision had been planned. Not
so with the poor squirrel! He sprang up on the

highest box, stretching straight up on his hind
legs, with fore paws pressed against his breast
and ears erect, his heart beating his sides and his
tail hanging down shamefacedly as he looked
anxiously toward the spruce where the blue jay
had gone. Gradually the fear on his face changed
to a comical look of bewilderment. Could that
bird flying about as if nothing had happened be
what struck him, or had he gone to sleep over his
corn and had a bad dream? He settled down on
his haunches with an expression of inane confusion, and finally turned back into his corn box, a
sorry contrast to the clear-headed blue jay.

This was the first morning the jays came, and
we were greatly entertained watching the development of affairs. There were only three birds
that were regular patrons of the corn barrel res-
taurant, while there were thirteen gray squirrels,
and when the squirrels got over their first surprise they seemed to consider the jays an insig-
nificant minority. There were no claw-to-bill
tussles, for when a jay was eating on a corn box
by the side of the tree, and a squirrel ran down
the trunk right above him, and gave a jump that
promised to land him on the jay's head, the bird
would quietly fly off. But such meekness was no
sign of discomfiture. The jays came back as often
as they were driven away. If the squirrels ob-
jected to their eating on a corner of the box with
them, the jays would hop down on the snow and

pick up the corn the squirrels had scattered there. They were so persistent, and at the same time so dignified and peaceable, that the squirrels could not hold out against them ; and though for a time the birds took advantage of the squirrels' laziness and got a good breakfast mornings before the sleepy fur coats appeared, two or three weeks of 10°—20° below zero silenced the squirrel's last prior-claims argument and the jays were allowed to eat undisturbed from the same boxes with them.

But it is not only the squirrels that the blue jays dine with, for one day last winter the little three-year-old came running out of the dining-room in great excitement, crying, "Oh, grandpa! come quick ! There are three partridges, and one of them is a blue jay!" Indeed, the other day the blue jays quite took possession of the corn barrels that are the special property of the partridges. The barrels stand under the branches of a Norway spruce on either side of a snow-shoe path that runs from the house, and though the jays were self-invited guests, I could not help admiring the picture they made, they flying about and sitting on the barrels, the dark green of the boughs bringing out the handsome blue of their coats.

But the spot where I have found the blue jays most at home is in the dense coniferous forests of the Adirondacks. I shall never forget seeing a

flock of them on Black Mountain. From the top
of the mountain the wilderness looked like a sea
of forest-clad hills, with an occasional reef out-
lined by surf, for the largest lakes seemed like
tracery in the vast expanse of forest. The im-
pressive stillness was broken only by the rare
cries of a pair of hawks that circled over the
mountain; for the most part they soared, silent as
the wilderness below them. Coming down into
the forest primeval, where the majestic hemlocks
towered straight toward the sky, and their mas-
sive knotted roots bound down the granite bowl-
ders that showed on the mountain side — there we
found the blue jays in their home. A flock of
them lived together, feeding on wild berries and
beechnuts, sporting among the ferns and mosses,
and drinking from the brook that babbled along
near the trail. What a home our handsome birds
had chosen! But the memory of the spot is
dreary. Unmoved by the beauty of the scene, to
which the blue jays gave color and life ; unawed
by the *benedicite* of the hemlocks ; betraying the
trust of the friendly birds, the boy of the party
crept into their very home and shot down one
after another of the family as they stood resistless
before him. To-day the pitiful lament of the
brave old birds haunts me, for, forgetting to fear
for themselves, those that were left flew about in
wild distress, and their cries of almost human
suffering reached us long after we had left the
desecrated spot.

XX.

YELLOW-BIRD ; AMERICAN GOLDFINCH ; THISTLE-BIRD.

THROW yourself down among the buttercups and daisies some cloudless summer day and look up at the sky till its wondrous blueness thrills through you as an ecstacy. Then catch your breath and listen, while out of the air comes a clear fluid note of rapture. Ah ! there is the little goldfinch — a bit of the sun's own gold — sauntering through the air, rising and falling to

the rhythm of his own ♩♪ ♩♪♩ This way and

dee-ree   dee-ee-ree.

that he flits, at each call fluttering his wings and then letting himself float down on the air. Spring up from the meadow and follow him till down from the blue sky he comes to alight airily on a pink thistle - top. Then as he bends over and daintily plucks out the tiny seeds that would soon have been ballooning through the air, you can admire the glossy black cap, wings, and tail that touch off his slender gold form.

Who would ever take this fairy-like beauty for a cousin of our plain chippy and song sparrow? And yet — his bill and size and family traits are the same. Pigeon-hole No. 4 was marked "finches, sparrows, etc.," and he is one of the

finches. He seems near enough like the sparrows
too, when you think how unlike he is to the blackbirds and orioles of No. 3, or the swallows of No.
6, the catbird of No. 10, and the robin or bluebird of No. 14.

Even the chickadee from No. 12 is a strong
contrast to him. His slender frame fits him for

flying through the air, while the chickadee's
plump, fluffy figure is suited to flitting about tree-
trunks and branches. Early in the spring the
chickadee goes to the woods, and, using his pointed
bill as a pick-axe, picks out a nest hole in the side
of a stump or tree trunk. But the goldfinch
waits until July, and then, going to the nearest
orchard, chooses a plum or apple-tree crotch and
sets about making a basket to fit it. He peels

the bark from some slender weed for the outside,
and pilfers a thistle-top or the silk storeroom of
some other plant for a lining.

An old nest the children brought me last fall
had a veritable feather-bed of down in it, on top
of the usual silky lining, and it stuffed the cup so
full there seemed hardly room enough for the
eggs. It looked as if two or three whole thistle-
tops had been put in and matted down.

Last year a pair of goldfinches built in a plum-
tree by the side of a carriage drive, so low that
on tiptoe I could reach into the nest to count over
the eggs from day to day. And what dainty light
blue shells they had. Just as if bits of blue sky
had fallen into the nest! The mother-bird must
have guessed my delight in her treasures, for she
would sit quietly on a tree a few feet away with
an air that said quite plainly, " Are n't they dear
little eggs? You can look at them just as long
as you like. I 'll wait here till you get through!"

As the goldfinches nest so much later than
most birds, the young are barely out before the
warblers and other of the birds begin migrating.
I have seen the little ones teasing their father for
food late in September. One day I saw one fed
on the head of a big sunflower.

I am afraid Mr. Goldfinch is not a good dis-
ciplinarian, for his babies follow him around fluttering their wings, opening their mouths, and
crying *tweet-ee, tweet-ee, tweet-ee, tweet-ee,* with

an insistence that suggests lax family government. Some one should provide him with a bundle of timothy stalks! And yet who would have our fairy use the rod? Just listen to him some day as he flies away from his nest, singing over to himself in tones of exquisite love and tenderness his sweet *bay-bee, bay-ee-bee*, and you will feel that the little father has a secret better than any known to the birch.

Our goldfinch is not a musician when it comes to his long song. That is a canary jumble of notes whose greatest charm is its light-heartedness. But though he is not as finished a songster as the canary, during the summer he is much prettier, for then his yellow suit is richly trimmed with black markings. In September however he loses his beauty, and until the next April or May, when his perilous travels are over for the season, looks much like his plain little wife. His black trimmings are gone, and he has become flaxen-brown above and whitish-brown below, — quite commonplace.

In connection with this protective change in plumage the "Naturalist" gives an interesting instance of protective habit, in which the wise birds disguised themselves by the help of their bright summer coats. A flock of them were dining on top of the stalks of yellow mullein that covered the slope of the embankment by which the observer and his party passed. He says: "The mulleins were ranged in stiff files, like soldiers in yellow uniforms, and each bird as we passed remained motionless, looking like a continuation of the spike, of which one might easily be deceived into thinking it part and parcel. As soon as we had passed by, the birds were again busy, flitting from plant to plant, feeding on the seeds and enjoying themselves."

What a difference it makes in our thought of winter to know that our little goldfinch will never find it too cold to visit us. Being a vegetarian, his storehouse is always well filled, for if the snow covers the seeds he would gather from the brown weed tops, he goes to the alders in the swamp; and if they fail him he is sure to find plenty in the seeds of the hemlock, the spruce, and the larch.

XXI.

PHŒBE.

CLASSING the crow-blackbird, bobolink, and oriole together in No. 3 by their striking colors, and distinguishing the sparrows in No. 4 by their striped backs, the common flycatchers, who belong in our first pigeon-hole, No. 1, stand out as unstriped, dull, dark grayish birds, with light breasts. Mr. Burroughs describes them as "sharp-shouldered, big-headed, short-legged, of no particular color, of little elegance of flight or movement."

Knowing that the vocal organs of the flycatchers are undeveloped, you are not surprised by the
contrast they present to the sweet-voiced sparrows
and finches, the talkative catbird, and the bobolink, who is always bubbling over with song, nor
do you wonder at the abrupt call of the phœbe.
Although it resembles a jerking repetition of
phœ-be, *phœ-be*, it is not precisely what the word
would indicate. The first part of the call is comparatively clear, but the second is a longer rasping
note, with a heavily trilled *r*, making the whole
more like *phœ-ree*, *phœ-ree*.

When the birds first begin coming north you
hear this note. When you have traced it to its
source, — and it is an excellent habit to see every
bird whose notes attract your attention, — the dull
olive gray coat and the whitish vest, with its
tinge of pale yellow, are soon forgotten in watching the odd ways of the bird.

Somewhat longer than a song sparrow, — two
thirds as large as a robin, — he is strikingly unlike
the cheery, busy sparrow, or, in fact, like any of
the birds we have had. There he sits on a branch,
in an attitude that would shock the neat songsters.
His wings droop at his sides, and his tail hangs
straight down in the most negligent fashion. He
seems the personification of listlessness ; but, —
focus your glass on him, — his wings are vibrating,
and his tail jerks nervously at intervals. Suddenly
he starts into the air, snaps his bill loudly over an

unsuspecting insect he has been lying in wait for, and before you breathe settles back on the branch with a spasmodic jerk of the tail.

And now, as he sits looking for another victim, you have a good chance to note, through your glass, the peculiarities of the bill that gave such a resounding "click." Birds' bills are their tools, — the oriole's is long and pointed for weaving, the chickadee's short and strong to serve as a pickaxe; but when the nest does not call for a tool of its own the bill conforms to the food habits of the bird, — as the white man's needs are met by knife and fork, and the Chinaman's by chopsticks. So the bills of the robin and bluebird, you remember, are long, thin, and slender, — well fitted for a worm diet, — while the sparrows, who live mostly on seeds, have the short, stout, cone-shaped finch bill. In the same way flycatchers' bills are specially adapted for their use, that of catching the insects upon which they live. At the base there are long stiff bristles, and the upper half of the bill hooks over the lower so securely at the end that when an insect is once entrapped it has small chance of escape.

The phœbe is fond of building in a crotch of the piazza, on the beams of old sheds, and under bridges, apparently indifferent to the dust and noise of its position; but away from the immediate haunts of man it usually nests in caves or rocky ledges, and sometimes takes possession of the upturned roots of a fallen tree. I well remember finding a cave nest when we were children. We let ourselves down into the cave by a crevice in the lime rock, and after groping our way among the loose stones that made the floor, and — as our anxious fathers insisted — the roof of the cave, crawling along low passages, wedging between narrow walls, and hunting for stepping stones across the dark pools that reflected the glimmer of our candles, we suddenly came into a flood of daylight, — a crack in the rocks wide enough to make a dangerous pitfall for the horses and cows that grazed overhead, but chosen by the phœbes as the safest possible nook for rearing a brood of baby birds. Down the sides of this shaft the rain trickled, keeping the moss green and giving the tiny ferns strength to cling to the crannies of the rock. On a ledge just in reach of the tallest of us the wise pair of birds had built their nest, careless of the dark cavern below, and happy among the moss and ferns.

XXII.

KINGBIRD ; BEE MARTIN.

THE kingbird is noticeably smaller than the robin, but is larger and more compactly built than most of the flycatchers. The sobriety of his plain blackish coat and white vest are relieved by a colored patch that may sometimes be espied under his crest, and also by a white tip to his tail, which, when spread in flight, has the effect of a white crescent. He has a peculiar flight, holding his head up and using his wings in a labored way as if he were swimming. When looking for his dinner he often flutters obliquely into the air, displaying his shining white breast and fan-shaped tail to the best advantage.

All the disagreeable qualities of the flycatchers seem to centre in this bird. His note is a harsh, scolding twitter. His crown proclaims him king, not by right, but by might, — such a bickering pugilist, such a domineering autocrat he is. The crow's life becomes a plague when this tormentor gives chase ; and the smaller birds find themselves driven at the point of the bill from the fences they had considered public highways.

But whatever may be the exact limit of his quarrelsomeness it stops short at home ; old kingbirds are certainly tender guardians of their young. I once watched a pair in search of food. They flew down to the haycocks in the meadow near the orchard, sat there reconnoitring for a moment, and then jumped into the grass to snap up the insect they had discovered. Flying back to the young they flirted their wings and tails as they dropped the morsel into the gaping red throats, and in an instant were off again for a hunt in the air, or in another tree. And so they kept hard at work, looking everywhere till the

voràcious appetites of their infants were satisfied.
DeKay says of the kingbird's diet: "He feeds
on berries and seeds, beetles, canker-worms, and
insects of every description. By this, and by his
inveterate hostility to rapacious birds, he more
than compensates for the few domestic bees with
which.he varies his repast." To this DeKay adds
the interesting statement : " Like the hawks and
owls, he ejects from his mouth, in the shape of
large pellets, all the indigestible parts of insects
and berries."

XXIII.

WOOD PEWEE.

In size, coloring, and habit you will hardly distinguish the wood pewee from the phœbe, although the former is somewhat smaller. These
two birds stand apart from all the others we have
had. The chimney swift and barn swallow also
live on insects, but measure the difference in their
methods of hunting. The swift zigzags through
the air, picking up his dinner as he goes; the
swallow skims the rivers, and circles over the
meadows and through the sky, without so much
as an ungraceful turn of the wing to suggest that
he is dining. But the phœbe and the wood pewee lie in wait for their victims. They cunningly
assume indifference until the unwary gauzy-wing
floats within range, then spring on it, snap it up,
and fall back to wait for another unfortunate.

And when not hunting, how silent and motionless they sit, the phœbe on the ridgepole of a barn, the wood pewee on a twig in the flickering sunlight and shade of the green woods ; neither of them uttering more than an occasional note, and scarcely stirring unless to look over their shoulders.

Though the phœbe and wood pewee look so much alike, in reality they are as much at odds as a farmer and a poet. Unlike the nest of the phœbe, the wood pewee's is essentially woodsy and distinctive. It is an exquisite little structure, saddled on to a lichen-covered limb. Made of fine roots and delicate stems of grass and seed pods, it is covered with bits of lichen or moss glued on with saliva, so that like the humming-bird's nest it seems to be a knob on the branch. It is a shallow little nest, and the four richly crowned creamy eggs, though tiny enough in themselves, leave little room for the body of the brooding mother.

In temper the phœbe is so prosaic that we naturally connect it with the beams of barns and cow sheds ; while the wood pewee, associated with the cool depths of the forest, is fitted to inspire poets, and to stir the deepest chords of human nature with its plaintive, far-reaching voice.

It has moods for all of ours. Its faint, lisping

pe-ee

suggests all the happiness of domestic love and peace. At one moment its minor

come to me

with the liquidity of a " U " of sound ♪♩♪ is fraught with all the pathos and yearning of a desolated human heart. At another, its tender, motherly

dear-ie   dear-ie   dear

with which it lulls its little ones, is as soothing to the perplexed and burdened soul as the soft breathing of the wind through the pine needles, or the caressing ripple of the sunset-gilded waves of a mountain lake.

XXIV.

LEAST FLYCATCHER.

IF you have been in the country, or even in one of our smaller towns during the spring and summer, you may have noticed the reiteration of an abrupt call of two notes — *che-beck' che-beck'* coming from the apple-trees and undergrowth. If you have traced it you have discovered a small gray bird, in coat and habit a miniature of the phœbe and wood pewee, jerking not only his tail but his whole body with his emphatic call.

This small bird seems a piquant satire on the

days of tournament and joust, when knights
started out with leveled lances to give battle to
every one they met. He is a fearless little war-
rior, snapping his bill ominously as he charges,
full tilt, at his enemy.

Last summer on passing a thicket I heard this
snapping, together with loud calls of *che-beck'*,
and stopped to see what was happening. There,
in a low willow, I found a family of young sunning themselves while their mother brought them
their dinner. It seemed a most peaceable scene,
but a picket fence ran along just back of the willow, and I soon discovered that this was the tilt
yard. Whenever a song sparrow or pewee happened to light there and stretch its wings for a
sun bath, the fierce little mother would suddenly
appear, dart at the unoffending bird, and fairly
throw him off the fence with her abrupt onset.

After unseating her enemy she would fly off as
fast as she had come, career about in the air till
she had snapped up a fly or miller, dart back,
thrust it into one of the open mouths with a jab
that threatened to decapitate the little one, and
seemed to mean, " There, take it quick if you 've
got to have it," and with a flirt of the tail and
wings, before I had time for a second look, would
be off in hot pursuit of another insect.

I wanted to see if she would be afraid of me,
and so crept up by the fence, almost under the
baby birds. Two of them sat there side by side,

in the most affectionate manner, nestling down on
the branch with their soft white feathers fluffed
out prettily. They did not mind me, and closed
their eyes as if the warm sunlight made them
sleepy. All of a sudden their mother flew up to
one of them with a fly, but was so startled on seeing me that instead of giving it to him she sprang
up on top of his head and was off like a flash,
almost tumbling him off the branch, and leaving
him very much scared and bewildered. As soon
as her nerves recovered from the shock she came
back again and went on with her work as if I had
not been there. The father seemed to be as restless and pugnacious as the mother, and, if appear-
ances were to be trusted, was quarreling with his
neighbors in a tree near by, while his wife guarded
the picket and fed her young.

XXV.

RED-WINGED BLACKBIRD.

The large flocks of blackbirds seen coming
north in the spring are confusing at first, but by
careful observation you will soon be able to discriminate between them. Sometimes the crow
blackbird and the red-wing fly together, but they
more commonly go in separate flocks. At a distance, the flight of the two is perhaps the most
distinctive feature — the " keel-tail " steering ap-

paratus of the crow blackbird marking him anywhere. Then, though they both belong in the
same pigeon-hole, the keel-tailed is a half larger,
and the red-wing a trifle smaller than the robin.
Known more familiarly, the red-wing lacks the
noisy obtrusiveness of his awkward cousin, and
usually prefers the field to the dooryard.

Though as I write the roads are being broken
through the drifted snow by plough and kettle, as
I turn over the crumpled leaves of the small note-
book I have carried on so many tramps, the first
faint, penciled notes I find on the red-wing take
me back into May, and, in fancy, we are again
starting down the hill to the swampy meadows
where

" The red-wing flutes his *o-ka-lee*."

Did you ever see a meadow full of cowslips?
Here is the true field of the cloth of gold. It
looks as if father Sun had crumbled up sunbeams
and scattered the bits over the meadow! As you
sink into the soft wet ground, every few steps
bring you to a luxuriant clump of the tender
green plants lit up by flower cups of glistening
gold. Each bunch seems more beautiful than the
last, and, like a child, I would carry the whole
field full of flowers home in my arms! This sun-
garden is the red-wing's playground. As we stroll
along, he flies over our heads calling out *o-ka-lee*,
and then, with outstretched wings, soars slowly
down to the ground, where he sits and wags his
tail as fast as a catbird.

As Thoreau says, his red wing marks him as effectually as a soldier's epaulets. This scarlet shoulder cap is so striking against the bird's black coat that the careless observer does not notice its border of brownish yellow, even when it shades into white, as it does in some of the western species. With Madam Blackbird the contrast is not so great, for she is not as pure black as her husband, having brownish streaks that, even at a distance, give her a duller look ; and then her epaulets are more salmon than scarlet. Still the effect is pleasing, and it is only a matter of taste if we do not admire her as much as her spouse.

I was unable to go to the meadows during the nesting season, and the next notes I find in my book were taken in the middle of June. Then the young were hidden in the grass, and the old birds followed us from spot to spot, screaming loudly as they circled near us, or hovered low over our heads. Perhaps their cries were to warn their children, for, although there were three of us, and we examined carefully all the places where they showed the most concern, we succeeded in scaring up only one rusty-coated youngster.

Two weeks later, in the warm days of July, the red-wings seemed to have left the meadows for the trees that skirted the alder swamp, and families of old and young were sitting with their cousin grackles in the willows and on the rail fence, while some flew up as I walked through an

opening in the swamp where the cat-tails stood
guard, and the long-banded rushes soughed like
wind in a forest.

XXVI.

HAIRY WOODPECKER.

THE habits of the woodpecker family are more
distinctive, perhaps, than those of any group of
the birds we have been considering, and the most
superficial observer cannot fail to recognize its
members.

Woodpeckers — the very name proclaims them
unique. The robin drags his fish-worm from its
hiding place in the sod, and carols his happiness
to every sunrise and sunset; the sparrow eats
crumbs in the dooryard and builds his nest in a
sweetbriar; the thrushes turn over the brown
leaves for food and chant their matins among the
moss and ferns of the shadowy forest; the goldfinch balances himself on the pink thistle or yellow mullein top, while he makes them " pay toll "
for his visit, and then saunters through the air in
the abandonment of blue skies and sunshine ; the
red-wing flutes his *o-ka-lee* over cat-tails and cowslips ; the bobolink, forgetting everything else,
rollicks amid buttercups and daisies ; but the
woodpecker finds his larder under the hard bark
of the trees, and, oblivious to sunrise and sunset,

flowering marsh and laughing meadow, clings
close to the side of a stub, as if the very sun himself moved around a tree trunk!

But who knows how much these grave mono-
maniacs have discovered that lies a sealed book

to all the world besides? Why should we scorn
them? They are philosophers! They have the secret of happiness. Any bird could be joyous with
plenty of blue sky and sunshine, and the poets,
from Chaucer to Wordsworth, have relaxed their
brows at the sight of a daisy; but what does the
happy goldfinch know of the wonders of tree
trunks, and what poet could find inspiration in a
dead stub on a bleak November day? Jack Frost
sends both thrush and goldfinch flying south, and

the poets shut their study doors in his face, drawing their arm-chairs up to the hearth while they rail at November. But the wise woodpecker clings to the side of a tree and fluffing his feathers about his toes makes the woods reverberate with his cheery song, — for it is a song, and bears an important part in nature's orchestra. Its rhythmical *rat tap, tap, tap, tap*, not only beats time for the chickadees and nuthatches, but is a reveille that sets all the brave winter blood tingling in our veins.

There the hardy drummer stands beating on the wood with all the enjoyment of a drum major. How handsome he looks with the scarlet cap on the back of his head, and what a fine show the white central stripe makes against the glossy black of his back !

Who can say how much he has learned from the wood spirits ? What does he care for rain or blinding storm ? He can never lose his way. No woodsman need tell him how the hemlock branches tip, or how to use a lichen compass.

Do you say the birds are gone, the leaves have fallen, the bare branches rattle, rains have blackened the tree trunks ? What does he care ? All this makes him rejoice ! The merry chickadee hears his shrill call above the moaning of the wind and the rattling of the branches, for our alchemist is turning to his lichen workshop.

The sealed book whose pictures are seen only

by children and wood fairies opens at his touch.
The black unshaded tree trunks turn into enchanted lichen palaces, rich with green and gold
of every tint. The "pert fairies and the dapper
elves" have left their magic circles in the grass,
and trip lightly around the soft green velvet moss
mounds so well suited for the throne of their
queen. Here they find the tiny moss spears Lowell
christened, "Arthurian lances," and quickly arm
themselves for deeds of fairy valor. Here, too, are
dainty silver goblets from which they can quaff
the crystal globes that drop one by one from the
dark moss high on the trees after rain. And
there — what wonders in fern tracery, silver filigree and coral for the fairy Guinevere!

But hark! the children are coming — and off
the grave magician flies to watch their play from
behind a neighboring tree trunk. There they
come, straight to his workshop, and laugh in glee
at the white chips he has scattered on the ground.

They are in league with the fairies, too, and
cast magic spells over all they see. First they spy
the upturned roots of a fallen tree. It is a mountain! And up they clamber, to overlook their
little world. And that pool left by the fall rains.
Ha! It is a lake! And away they go, to cross
it bravely on a bridge of quaking moss.

As they pass under the shadow of a giant hemlock and pick up the cones for playthings, they
catch sight of the pile of dark red sawdust at the

foot of the tree and stand open-mouthed while the oldest child tells of a long ant procession she saw there when each tiny worker came to the door to drop its borings from its jaws. How big their eyes get at the story! If the woodpecker could only give his cousin the yellow hammer's tragic sequel to it!

But soon they have found a new delight. A stem of basswood seeds whirls through the air to their feet. They all scramble for it. What a pity they have no string! The last stem they found was a kite and a spinning air-top for a day's play. But this — never mind — there it goes up in the air dancing and whirling like a gay young fairy treading the mazes with the wind.

" Just see this piece of moss ! How pretty ! " And so they go through the woods, till the brown beech leaves shake with their laughter, and the gray squirrels look out of their oriel tree trunk windows to see who goes by, and the absorbed magician — who can tell how much fun he steals from his lofty observation post to make him content with his stub !

Why should he fly south when every day brings him some secret of the woods, or some scene like this that his philosopher's stone can turn to happiness ? Let us proclaim him the sage of the birds !

If he could speak ! The children would gather about him for tales of the woodsprites ; the student of trees would learn facts and figures enough

to store a book; and the mechanic! Just watch
the dexterous bird as he works!

A master of his trade, he has various methods.
One day in September he flew past me with a
loud scream, and when I came up to him was
hard at excavating. His claws were fast in the
bark on the edge of the hole, and he seemed to be
half clinging to it, half lying against it. His stiff
tail quills helped to brace him against the tree,
and he drilled straight down, making the bark fly
with his rapid strokes. When the hole did not
clear itself with his blows, he would give a quick
scrape with his bill and drill away again. Suddenly he stopped, picked up something, and flew
up on a branch with it. He had found what he
was after. And what a relish it proved! I could
almost see him holding it on his tongue.

Another day in November he had to work
harder for his breakfast, and perhaps it was fortunate. The night before there had been a sharp
snowstorm from the north, so that in passing
through the woods all the trees and undergrowth
on the south of me were pure white, while on the
opposite side the gray trees with all their confusion of branches, twigs, and noble trunks stood out
in bold relief. The snow that had fallen made it
rather cold standing still, and I would have been
glad to do part of Mr. Hairy's work myself. But
he needed no help. He marched up the side of
the stub, tapping as he went, and when his bill

gave back the sound for which he had been listening, he began work without ado. This bark must have been harder or thicker than the other, for instead of boring straight through, he loosened it by drilling, first from one side and then from the other. When he could not get it off in this way, he went above, and below, to try to start it, so that, before he found his worm he had stripped off pieces of bark several inches long and fully two across. He was so much engrossed that I came to the very foot of the stub without disturbing him.

Indeed, woodpeckers are not at all shy here but work as unconcernedly by the side of the house as anywhere else. Once I was attracted by the cries of a hairy, and creeping up discovered a mother feeding her half-grown baby. She flew off when she saw me, probably warning the little fellow to keep still, for he stayed where she left him for five or ten minutes as if pinioned to the branch, crouching close, and hardly daring to stir even his head. Then, as she did not come back, and he saw no reason to be afraid of me, he flew off independently to another limb, and marched up the side arching his neck and bowing his head as much as to say, " Just see how well I walk ! "

XXVII.

DOWNY WOODPECKER.

THE downy looks so much like the hairy that it would be easy to confound them if it were not for the difference in size. The downy is fully two inches shorter than the hairy. As you see him on a tree at a distance, the white stripe on his back is bounded by black, or as Thoreau expresses it, "his cassock is open behind, showing his white robe." Above this stripe is a large check of black and white, and below on a line with the tips of his wings seems to be a fine black and white check, while, if he is an adult male, a scarlet patch on the back of his head sets off his black and white dress.

Seen only a rod away, as I see him through the window in winter, clinging to a tree, and picking at the suet hung out for him, the white central stripe of his back is marked off above by a black line which goes across to meet the black of his shoulders. From the middle of this and at right angle to it, another black line goes straight up towards his head, so carrying on the line of the white stripe, and forming the dividing line of the two white blocks. This, again, meets the point of a black V, so broad as to be almost a straight line. On this V lies the red patch of the back of his head. Over his eye is a white line that extends back to meet the red patch. What at a distance looked like fine checking at the base of his wings proves to be white lining across the black.

The downy comes about us here with the same familiarity as the hairy, and it was only a few weeks ago that the cook brought me one she found imprisoned between the sashes of her window. He was scared, poor little fellow, and wriggled excitedly, trying to force my hand open. When I had taken a look at his pretty brown eyes I carried him to the front door, and off he flew to the nearest tree where he began pecking at the bark as if nothing had happened.

XXVIII.

WHITE-BELLIED NUTHATCH ; DEVIL-DOWN HEAD.

CROSSBILLS, snow buntings, blue jays, pine finches, pine grosbeaks, goldfinches, and sometimes other birds visit us here at irregular intervals during the winter, but there are four little friends that never desert us, no matter how long the winter lasts. They form a novel quartette, for the chickadee *whistles* the air, the nuthatch sings his meagre alto through his nose, and the two woodpeckers — the hairy and downy — beat their drums as if determined to drown the other parts. But they are a merry band, with all their oddities, and wander about giving concerts wherever they go, till the woods are alive again, and we forget that we have ever missed the summer birds.

When the drums get too much absorbed in their tree trunks, the alto and air go serenading by themselves, and who knows what gossip they indulge in about the grave magicians' day dreams, or how gayly they swear to stand by each other and never be put down by these drums! They are old chums, and work together as happily as Mr. and Mrs. Spratt, the chickadee whistling his merry *chick-a-dee-dee, dee, dee* as he clings to a twig in the tree *top*, and the nuthatch answering back with a jolly little *yank, yank, yank*, as he hangs, head down, on the side of a tree *trunk*. What a comic figure he makes there!

Trying to get a view of you, he throws his head back and stretches himself away from the tree till you wonder he does not fall off. His black cap and slate-blue coat are almost hidden, he raises his white throat and breast up so high.

" Devil-down-head " he is called from this habit of walking down the trees, since instead of walking straight down backwards, as the woodpeckers do, he prefers to obey the old adage and "follow his nose." A lady forgetting his name once aptly described him to me as " that little upside-down bird," for he will run along the under side of a branch with as much coolness as a fly would cross the ceiling.

One of his popular names is "sapsucker," for our nuthatch has a sweet tooth, and when the farmers tap the trees in spring he "happens round" at the sugar bush to see what sort of maple syrup they are to have. He tests it well, taking a sip at "the calf" where it oozes out from

the gashing of the axe, tasting it as it dries along the spile, and finally on the rim of the buckets.

But his most interesting name is — *nuthatch!* How does he come by it? That seems a riddle. Some cold November day put on a pair of thick boots and go to visit the beeches. There in their tops are the nuthatches, for they have deserted the tree trunks for a frolic. They are beechnutting! And that with as much zest as a party of school-children starting out with baskets and pails on a holiday. Watch them now! What clumsy work they make of it, trying to cling to the beechnut burr and get the nuts out at the same time. It's a pity the chickadee can't give them a few lessons! They might better have kept to their tree trunks. But they persist, and after tumbling off from several burrs, finally snatch out a nut and fly off with it as calmly as if they had been dancing about among the twigs all their days. Away they go till they come to a maple or some other rough-barked tree, when they stick the nut in between the ridges of the bark, hammer it down, and then, when it is so tightly wedged that the slippery shell cannot get away from them, by a few sharp blows they *hatch* the *nut* from the tree! Through my glass I watched a number of them this fall, and they all worked in about the same way, though some of them wedged their nuts far into cracks or holes in the body of the tree, instead of in the bark. One of them pounded so hard he spread his tail and almost upset himself. The fun was so great a downy woodpecker tried it, and of all the big school-boys! The excitement seemed to turn his head, and he attacked a beechnut burr as if he would close with it in mortal combat!

Though without any real song, the nuthatch has a delightful variety of notes. In May his nasal *henk-a, henk-a, henk-a,* comes through the

soft green woods as a peculiarly peaceful caressing note, and his soft *yang, yang, yang* is full of
woodsy suggestions. In the last of June I noted
the sweet *yah-ha* of the nuthatch, the same *yang,
yang, yang*, and his nearest approach to a song,
the rapid *yah-ha, ha-ha-ha-ha.* In August and
September the nasal *yank* is sometimes run into
an accelerated half song. Thoreau gives the ordinary winter note as *quah, quah*, and while that
expresses the mellowness of the note on some
days better than *yank*, they are both descriptive.
But though certain notes may predominate in
given months, on a cold January morning I have
heard from a flock of nuthatches every note that
I had ever heard before at any time of the year.
Like the other members of the quartette, the nuthatch nests in holes in trees or stumps while its
lightly spotted eggs, six or eight in number, are
laid on a soft, felty lining.

I am often surprised by discovering the nuthatch at work in places where I despair of finding
any birds. One day in December the snow-cov-
ered woods seemed to have fallen into the silent
slumber of a child. Not a breath came to blow
the white cap from the vireo's nest, or scatter the
heaped-up snow that rested like foam on the slender twigs. The snow that had drifted against the
side of the tree trunks clung as it had fallen. In
silence the branches arched under their freight;
the rich ochraceous beech leaves hung in masses
under the snow — not a leaf rustled.

Overhead the twigs, snow-outlined, made exquisite filigree against the pale blue sky. But suddenly, as the woods seemed to be holding its breath, the *yank* of the nuthatch came first from one tree and then another. A family of them were looking for their dinner in the white forest. If the snow covered the upper side of a branch, they ran along upside-down on the under side; if the south side of a tree trunk was white, they walked, head down, on the north side; and there, too, was the little drummer — a downy woodpecker, flickering from tree to tree — even here, the merry band was finding a place for itself in nature. As I passed on, fainter and fainter came the note of the nuthatch. I looked back through the woods; the blue sky was veiled by snow clouds, but behind them shone the southern sun, pervading them with that wondrous radiance of white light that only a winter sky can show.

XXIX.

COWBIRD.

THE cowbird is one of the smaller blackbirds. The male has an iridescent body and purplish-brown head and neck. The female has no brilliant coloring, and is decidedly dingy in appearance.

About the size of the kingbird, the cowbird imposes upon its brothers in the same systematic manner. It employs subtle measures, however, and the result of its work is much worse than that of the kingbird. Audubon says, " Like some un-natural parents of our own race, it sends out its progeny to be nursed." Coues says of its habits : " Like the European cuckoo, it builds no nest, laying its eggs by stealth in the nests of various other birds, especially warblers, vireos, and spar-rows ; and it appears to constitute, furthermore, a remarkable exception to the rule of conjugal affection and fidelity among birds. A wonderful provision for the perpetuation of the species is seen in its instinctive selection of smaller birds as the foster-parents of its offspring ; for the larger egg receives the greater share of warmth during incubation, and the lustier young cowbird asserts its precedence in the nest ; while the foster-birds, however reluctant to incubate the strange egg (their devices to avoid the duty are sometimes astonishing), become assiduous in their care of the foundling, even to the neglect of their own young. The cowbird's egg is said to hatch sooner than that of most birds ; this would obviously con-fer additional advantage."

The birds upon which the cowbird imposes sometimes build a second floor to their houses when they find the big stranger egg in their home, and a case is given where even a third story was built. The cowbird spends a large share of his time among the cattle in the pastures, so earning his name.

With the cowbird, our pigeon-hole for "blackbirds, orioles, etc.," No. 3, is as full as we shall make it. There are seven birds in it — the bobolink, cowbird, red-winged blackbird, meadow-lark, crow-blackbird, and oriole. Comparing them for a moment with the lower orders of birds we put away in the drawer — the chimney swift, partridge, humming-bird, cuckoo, woodpeckers, and kingfisher; and then again with the other families of perching birds we have had — the flycatchers of No. 1, the finches and sparrows of No. 4, the barn swallow from No. 6, and the chickadee and nuthatch from the "nuthatches and tits" of No. 12, we shall see how clearly they stand out as a group.

Perhaps it will be well to summarize their common characteristics.

BLACKBIRDS, ORIOLES, etc.   (Pigeon-hole No. 3.)

Birds that live in the meadows.
>   Meadow-lark.
>   Bobolink.

Birds with much black in plumage.   (Compare with sparrows.)
>   Crow blackbird.
>   Red-winged blackbird.
>   Cowbird.
>   Bobolink.
>   Oriole.

Birds whose general build is compact but slender, and by whom the claw is used for holding food. (Compare with robin and sparrows.)

> Oriole.
> Crow blackbird.
> Red-winged blackbird.

Birds in which the females are smaller than the males.

> Red-winged blackbird.
> Cowbird.
> Meadow-lark.
> Crow blackbird.

Birds with long straight bills. (Compare with swift, chickadee, finches, and sparrows.)

> Crow blackbird.
> Red-winged blackbird.
> Meadow-lark.
> Oriole.

Birds that walk instead of hopping. (Compare with flycatchers, sparrows, etc.)

> Crow blackbird.
> Red-winged blackbird.
> Cowbird.
> Meadow-lark.

XXX.

WHITE-THROATED SPARROW.

THOUGH the white-throats nest in the Adirondacks and other dense northern forest regions, they
come to us for only about a month in spring and
fall.   In Northampton, Massachusetts, I have
heard their clear spring whistles, —

I - I - pea - bod - dy, pea-bod - dy, pea - bod - dy

I - I - I - pea - bod - dy,   pea - bod - dy

coming from the wooded bank of Mill River, from
the low bushes of the fields, and the undergrowth
of the woods on the outskirts of the city ; and in
the fall have seen them in front of the houses
scratching among the leaves under the evergreens
of Round Hill.

The first intimation I had of their return this
fall was in the clearing one day, when I found two
of them sitting atilt of a blackberry bush in front
of me.   As one of them sat facing me and the
other had his back to me and only turned to look
over his shoulder, I had a chance to note not only
the white chin and ash-gray breast but the black
striped chestnut back and the pretty five-striped
crown, whose central grayish line is enclosed by

two black lines, bounded in turn by the whitish line over the eyes. While I was watching them their attention was diverted by the barking of a gray squirrel in the woods, but they seemed to listen to him as they had me, with quiet interest, little more.

A large flock of them stayed here for about a month, keeping always near the same spots, — a brush heap, an old dead tree-top, by which water and grain were kept for them, and a raspberry patch a few rods away. From the raspberry patch would come their quarrying note that Mr. Bicknell speaks of, the peculiar *chelink* that gives the sound of a chisel slipping on stone, and which, when coming from a flock at a little distance, gives the effect of a quarry full of stone cutters. As I went through the patch they would fly up from among the bushes, some uttering a little surprised *chree*, some calling *cheep* as they flew noisily by, while others clung, crouching close, to the side of a stem, looking back to see who I was.

The small slate-colored snowbirds, the juncos, were with the sparrows more than any other birds ; but the oven-bird, whose premises they had invaded, looked down on them with mild curiosity until it was time for her to go south ; and later, a family of chewinks chased them off the fence by way of turnabout justice, though you are tempted to feel that the white-throats need little punishment. They have none of the petulance or arbitrariness of chippy, but with the sweet temper of the song sparrow, these larger cousins have a thoughtful bearing that harmonizes with their spring song, which is tinged with sadness, like the melodious call of the bluebird.

One morning in September, not finding the white-throats in the raspberry-patch, I went on to a circular opening near the edge of the woods just south of it. The sunlight streaming down through the half Indian summer haze and melting into the soft lights and shadows of the surrounding green woods, gave a mystic loveliness to the spot. A delicate white birch stretched up, sunning itself; a maple trunk stood in shadow with one spray of a drooping branch dipped in the emerald sun dye; the red autumn leaves lodged here and there seemed to be shaken out of sight by the green bushes, but a breath of fresh wind murmured that summer was past and — was it a footstep? No! It was an army of little autumn pedestrians! A happy host of white-throated sparrows, hopping about on the ground under the bushes. Busy and fearless, their footsteps pattered on the leaves, and they sometimes came within two or three feet of me without taking fright. A chipmunk scudded through the bushes after his playfellow without startling them. From every side came the happy *chee-ree;* a cobweb shimmered in the sunlight. What if fall *were* coming? It brought these little friends of ours!

XXXI.

CEDAR-BIRD; WAXWING.

THE cedar-birds go into pigeon-hole No. 7, the place for "the waxwings," etc., and when you have examined them you will feel that they deserve a cubby-hole of their own. In spring and fall they are found in flocks, often of five or seven, but you will be likely to overlook them if you are not consciously watching the birds. They are rather shy, and are slender birds, a little smaller than a robin, with inconspicuous coloring, and, moreover, have no song to attract your attention, — nothing but a lisping note and a faint whistle that sounds as if they were drawing in their breath. But they are about, and in June will probably nest in the nearest orchard, and eat canker-worms from the village trees.

When you find them you will be repaid for your trouble. By the law of compensation, discussed by Darwin under the head of Natural Selection, their beauty makes up for their lack of voice, while, in the case of the sparrows, plainness is compensated by musical power.

The waxwing's plumage is a soft fawn tone, lit up by touches of color. Its crest is fawn, but it has a black chin and a black stripe through the eye, a yellow band across the end of its tail, and, — most unique external feature of all, which ex-

plains the name waxwing — a tipping of a bright
red horny substance that looks like sealing-wax
on the shorter feathers of its wings, and sometimes the feathers of the tail. How prettily the
tipping lights up its dainty coat! It gives the
final touches to an artistic costume. But what
impresses you most at first sight is the waxwing's
crest, and the fact that, unlike the fluffy chickadee, every delicately tinted feather of its shapely
body is smoothed into place with exquisite care.
The waxwings are the élite of bird circles, and
seem fit companions for the proud oriole and the
graceful catbird. But how modest and retiring
they seem as they hide away among the leaves,
silent and self-contained, while the handsome oriole
flaunts his scarlet banner through the air, blowing
a bugle-note for all the world to hear; and the
gay Bohemian catbird chuckles at his own jokes,
and tells the lilacs all he knows as he idles in the
sunshine.

Nuttall relates a curious instance of politeness
which he noticed among cedar-birds. One, having caught an insect, gave it to his neighbor, who
took it to give to another, he in turn passing it on,
till it had gone the rounds of the group before it
was devoured!

The gentle affectionate nature of the cedar-bird
has often been commented upon, and naturalists
have called attention to the fact that the pretty
little birds have even adopted the human symbol

of tenderness, and are often seen kissing each other. Gumpei Kuwada, the young Japanese observer at Northampton, Massachusetts, has sent me some interesting notes on the subject. He says : " On the 7th of May I saw a very large flock of cedar-birds, *Ampelis cedrorum*. Two of these were seated on a branch a little distance apart, and one hopped toward the other and bent down his head and touched the bill of the other with his own bill, then went back to his place; then the second bird went to the first bird and went through the same motions and returned to his place; then the first bird repeated the performance, and so these two cedar-birds went alternately and touched each other's bills for about five minutes. The action of the two birds was so funny that I could not call it anything else but that they fell in love and kissed each other. It could not possibly have been a mother feeding her young, because it was so early in the season, and they were in a flock and had nothing in their bills, and their bills were shut."

The cedar-birds are not only affectionate in their own families, but sometimes show the most human compassion to stranger birds. Mrs. Martha D. Jones, of Northampton, writes me of a touching instance of their friendliness. She says : " Last summer my sister watched for weeks a robin's nest in an apple-tree some ten feet from her chamber window. She could see into the nest,

and day by day watched the maturing of love and
hope and faith till the little ones were fledged.
Then came a sad day when the mother bird was
killed, and again a sadder still when the sole pro-
vider of the hungry brood was taken. Who
should provide for the four little gaping mouths?
Must the little ones perish also? Their pitiful
cries could be heard in the house, and my sister
tried to devise some way to reach the nest and
relieve them. When lo! she was anticipated.
The young had been heard, and a pitiful heart
had responded. . . . A cedar-bird came before
the day closed and adopted them, fed them constantly for more than a week; brought them
safely from the nest and taught them to fly as
though they had been her own." What an example these birds could set the kingbird and
least flycatcher!

XXXII.

CHEWINK ; TOWHEE.

THE sight of a chewink, even in migration, is
a rare pleasure in the Adirondack region. One
October morning when the orchard trees and
evergreens are astir with sparrows, a big umber-
brown bird comes out from the low branches of a
Norway spruce, and, showing white tail feathers
as she flies, hides away among the low spreading

branches of a white birch. Just as I begin to
question my eyes, she flies into a plum-tree and I
recognize the small brown head, the short finch
bill, — for she belongs in pigeon-hole No. 4, — and
the white triangular corners of the chewink tail.

But on the instant she spies me, and away she flies,
low over the ground to — I never know where.
Had she clapped on a magic cap she could not
have vanished more completely. I waste the best
part of the morning hunting for her, and the next
day begin the search again.

Going along a narrow trail that serves as snow-
shoe path in winter, in passing a dead tree top I
start the usual number of white-throats, and as I
turn the corner of the fence into the clearing — behold! — right before me, clinging to the side of a

raspberry stem and looking at me over his shoulder, is a handsome male chewink. What a beauty! His back is black and his sides match the crisp curled beech leaves that color the wood paths in fall. He whisks his tail back and forth, and opens and shuts it as a nervous beauty toys with her fan, so disclosing the white feathers that border it and the white triangles on the corners. But before I can put pencil to note-book he has disappeared. I spy about in all directions, get down on my knees to peer through the raspberry bushes, and tiptoe along, ogling all the white-throats that light on the fence — but never a glimpse do I get of him.

Then suddenly he appears on top of a fence facing me; but as I look down he hops among the ferns, and as I screen myself behind a tree for a better view when he shall fly up again, a low *cheree-ah-ree* reaches me, and I see him on the fence several rods away! He looks up to the trees, raising and lowering his cap, with the odd effect of rounding or flattening his head, and then, deciding in favor of brambles, jumps off into the bushes again.

And so I follow him for three or four hours, trying every device to keep near without letting him take fright, stepping on moss or walking along the trunks of fallen trees to avoid the crackling sound of the leaves, stopping to listen for his soft *cheree-ah-ree*, getting down to look through the bare stems of the bushes for him, and, if I see him as he scratches among the leaves, crouch motionless close to the ground till I am as full of cramps as Caliban. Once, seeing him on the fence, I stand close to a tree and take an old dry golden-rod — curious freak it is too, with axillary flowers all the way up the stem — and hang it from a twig in front of me as a screen and in that way get a good look at him through my glass.

Off his guard, he loses the alert nervous manner noticed at first, and seems winningly peaceful and social — but just as I am allowing him all the virtues of the decalogue, he flies at a white-throat that presumes to light on the fence, and drives it off in a temper!

I next find both Mr. and Mrs. Chewink by the corner of the fence where grain and water are kept for the birds, and when Mr. Chewink is not chasing after white-throats, they busy themselves hunting among the leaves. Near by a partridge sits motionless on a limb, so close to a tree she seems part of it. So much for being in the landscape! I take Madam Partridge's hint, and perch myself on the fence with my back to a tree that stands by it; and, thanks to the device, when Mr. Chewink comes, after hopping about unconsciously just in range of my glass, he flies up on an arching blackberry stem only a few feet from me and sings softly to himself for several minutes without ever noticing me!

After about a week a storm came that drove

the chewinks south, and I searched through the raspberry patch and wandered through the woods calling to them in vain. But one day after the middle of the month I found another male eating the grain. He scratched among the leaves in full view, running at them with a queer energetic motion, tossing them up behind him. I had a long conversation with him, but though he answered all my remarks in a very friendly way, he looked cold, and talked in rather a pensive strain, and I saw no more of the family that fall.

XXXIII.

INDIGO-BIRD.

In a paper in the " Audubon Magazine," Mr. Ridgway has shown what a mistake has been made in depreciating our American songsters. With equal justice an article might be written, calling attention to the brilliant plumages of many of our northern birds. The purple grackle, oriole, bluebird, goldfinch, humming-bird, barn swallow, blue jay, purple finch, scarlet tanager, red-headed woodpecker, yellow-throated vireo, and numbers of our warblers would excite wondering delight if they should bear South American or European labels. Indeed, among birds as among roadside flowers, we need to make it the fashion to appreciate our own national gallery of beauties.

Not the least of our most brilliant every-day songsters is the indigo-bird. Only in a poor light is he as dull as common indigo. In the sunlight his coat is an intense, exquisite blue, the shade of which varies as he moves, and is described by Thoreau as " glowing indigo." Mrs. Indigo has a pretty tinge of blue on her shoulders and tail feathers, but if the light is not right to bring this out, the peculiarly warm brown, which is almost burnt sienna, is enough to distinguish her from the ordinary brown birds that are like her in size and build. Her habit of jerking her tail from side to side is also diagnostic.

The indigo-bird is one of our most energetic, tireless songsters. He is usually seen on the top of a bush or a tree not more than twenty or thirty feet high ; often in the edge of the woods, or in a clump of bushes beside the road, and sometimes in the garden, where his breezy, sunny song shows that he is making the most of all the light and air that are to be had. Blithe and merry in the sunshine, he sings as loudly through the noonday heat as in the cooler hours.

His roundelay has been syllabified in various ways, but the rhythm and tone may be suggested by *che-ree' che-ree' che-ree' che-ree' che-rah' rah-rup'.* The last half varies greatly, sometimes being *che-rah' rah-ah-rup,* or *che-rah' che-rip' cherup'.* Very often the song ends with an indescribable, rapid flourish of confused notes.

This June a pair of indigo-birds built in the edge of the woods only a few rods from the house, but I think they never ceased to regret their temerity. The nest was a pretty little bunch of dry leaves and grass, and its deep, narrow cavity was lined with hair. It was wedged into the fork of a tiny beech, only six inches from the ground, and not more than three feet from the carriage drive. The mother would sit quietly when wagons passed, but as soon as she found that I had discovered her nest would fly off in distress whenever I happened to be walking by. Unlike goldfinches and sparrows, the mother never got used to me, and to the last suspected me of — I don't know what murderous intentions — darting off into the low bushes with her metallic *cheep, cheep,* as soon as she caught sight of me, and almost refusing to feed her babies till I had gone back to the house. Her husband, though somewhat suspicious, could not share her alarm; he chirped and jerked his tail about, but his anxiety had a perfunctory air.

Earlier in the season I saw a very marked instance of this difference in temperament. I was walking through the edge of a clearing when I scared up a mother indigo-bird, apparently looking for a good site for her nest. She was much excited, and twitched her tail as she flew about crying *cheep, cheep.* She made so much noise that her husband heard her, and came flying home to rescue her. He did not think either my dogs or

I looked belligerent, but followed her from limb to limb to be near if we should attack her. It was evident that he did not sympathize with her fears, as he neither cried out nor jerked his tail; and after he had chased her patiently all over the branches, from one tree to another, and through the bushes, at last he turned toward her on a branch and looked at her as much as to say, —

"Oh! you tiresome creature; why will you be so absurd? Don't you see they're not going to hurt you?"

His contempt had no effect, however, and — he opened his mouth at her! This threat of conjugal authority subdued her, and at last she meekly flew off into the woods with him. But, like some other good wives, she had her way in the end, and though she followed Mr. Indigo back there several times to look for "empty lots," two or three more scares determined her, and the nest was built elsewhere!

XXXIV.

PURPLE FINCH.

THE purple finch is about the size of his cousin the song sparrow. He is as fond of singing in a maple or an evergreen as chippy is of trilling on the lawn, and the result is much more satisfactory, although he does not sing as well as the song sparrow.

Now and then you catch a sweet liquid note, but for the most part his song is only a bright warble, without beginning or end. The song sparrow, you know, begins, strikes his upper note three times, and then runs down the scale, finishing off usually with a little flourish ; but the purple finch seems to sing in circles, without much musical sense — nothing but a general feeling that the sun is warm and bright, and there are plenty of buds and seeds to be found near by. Thoreau puts the song in syllables as — *a-twitter-witter-witter-wee, a-witter-witter-wee.*

The song is at its best when our pretty finch is in love. Then it has more expression and sweetness and resembles the whisper song of the robin. And when he bows and dances before the little brown lady he is trying to win for his bride, his pretty magenta head and back, his rosy throat and white breast, with his graceful ways and tender song, make him an attractive suitor. The brown-streaked, sparrowy-looking little creature who seems to ignore him at first, can scarcely help feeling flattered by the devotion of such a handsome cavalier, and you feel sure that his wooing will come to a happy end.

Like the waxwings, bobolinks, white-throated sparrows, blue jays, goldfinches, and swifts, except in the nesting season, the purple finches are generally found in flocks, their favorite haunts being woods and orchards.

XXXV.

RED-EYED VIREO.

AMONG the songs that come through the open window in summer, there is one I hear when the midday heat has silenced nearly all the others. It comes from the upper branches of the trees about the house, and is a preoccupied warble of three loud, guttural notes, given with monotonous variety. In rhythm it is something like *he-ha-wha* or *ha-ha-wha*, or, again, *he-ha-whip* in rising inflection, and *he-ha-whee* in falling cadence.

If I go out and focus my glass on the dull-colored bird that moves along over the branches inspecting the leaves in such a business-like way, I discover it to be an exquisite little creature, tinted more delicately than the waxwing, but with much the same glossy look and elegant air. It is a slender bird, about half as large as a robin. Its back is olive, and its breast white, of such tints that when the sunlight is on the leaves our vireo is well disguised, for its back looks like the upper side of the leaf, and its breast like the under side with the sun on it. If the bird considerately flies down into the lower branches, as it turns its head to one side, I can make out its ash-colored cap and the lines that border it, — first a black one, then a white, and below that another black line, running through the eye.

If its search among the lower branches is suc-
cessful it runs along the length of a limb, holding
its worm out at bill's length, shaking it over the
limb as if afraid of dropping it before it is in con-
dition to swallow.

But although one becomes attached to the cheery
bird that sings at its work from morning till night,
in park and common, as well as about the country
house, the best way to know it is to follow one of
the family into the edge of the woods where it
builds its nest.

Such an exquisite little workman as you discover
it to be! It wonders how the meadow-lark and
bobolink can like to nest on the damp ground, and
how the woodpeckers can live in a tree trunk, —
how can they ever keep their babies quiet without
a cradle! The coarse mud-plastered house of the
robin fills it with lofty surprise. For its part it
usually chooses a lithe sapling that responds to all
the caprices of the wind, and from the fork of one
of its twigs hangs a dainty birch-bark basket.

For lining it picks up leaf-bud cases, curving
stems of the maple seeds, — wings the children
call them, — and now and then a spray of hemlock. With the artist's instinct it puts the strips
of brown bark next the lining, and keeps the shining silvery bits for the outside. Sometimes it
puts in pieces of white, crisp, last year's leaves,
and often steals the side of a small wasp's nest to
weave in with the rest, while bits of white cob-

web-like substance that look as if taken from co-
coons are fastened on for ornament.

What could you have more daintily pretty?
Nothing after the four white, delicately wreathed
oval eggs are laid on the maple wing stems in the
bottom.

On such a nest as this, with the tender green
leaves to shield her from stray sunbeams, and the
wind to rock her gently back and forth, brooding
must lose some of its wearisome monotony; and
you are tempted to account for the difference between the nervousness of some bird mothers and
the contented trustfulness of the vireo.

One day I accidentally surprised a vireo on her
nest. Here was a chance to see her red eyes. I
leveled my glasses at them and stared with the in-
sistent curiosity of an enthusiast. Nearer and
nearer I crept, and actually got within two feet of
the tree before she stirred. Then she flew off
with only a mildly complaining *whee-ough*, and
sat down in a tree near by to see what I would do
next. But just then I espied a wasp's nest about
two feet over hers, and not waiting to see if it was
" to let," retreated, wondering at the proximity.

There were a number of vireo families that I
was watching last spring, and one of them built
so low that by pulling down the end of the branch
I could reach into the nest. One day when I
went to examine the eggs they had turned into a
family of such big yellow-throated youngsters that
they filled the nest.

The mother did not seem to be there, so I sat down with my dogs near by to wait for her. I supposed she was off worm-hunting and would fly back in great excitement on discovering the intruders. But all at once, almost over my head, I heard a low, crooning *whee-ah!* I turned in surprise, and there was my mother bird looking down at me with all the composure of an old friend. *Wha-wha-wha*, she said, as she saw the dogs and took in the group again. As we kept still, and did not offer to molest her children, she soon began looking about for worms, saying *ter-ter-eater* in the most complacent tone as she worked. She would turn her head and look down at us now and then with mild curiosity; but although I went back to the nest to test her she seemed to have perfect confidence in me, not showing the least alarm.

Afterward I heard the vireo song from her, and concluded that *she* was the *father* of the family, left on guard while the mother was taking her rest. I thought perhaps that accounted for some of the indifference, but after that, when I went to see them, I found both old birds, and always met with the same trustfulness. Indeed, they would talk to me in the most friendly manner, answering my broken bird talk with gentle sympathetic seriousness that said very plainly they knew I meant well, and what a sweet winsome sound it had, uttered in their low caressing tones!

To their enemies, however, these beautiful birds are neither gentle nor confiding. Last June, as I was watching a chestnut-sided warbler from the undergrowth near a vireo's nest, I heard a great commotion among the thrushes and vireos, and hurried out of the cover to see what was the trouble. I heard a low complaining croon from one of the vireos, and looking up saw, to my surprise, a gray screech owl flying blindly about among the branches. After a little he stumbled upon a dead limb and sat down, trying to feel at home. But the vireos were crying ominously *kray, kree-kree-kree-kree*, and when he thought how they had darted down and snapped their bills at him as he came along, he edged uneasily over the branch. Just then my dog came running noisily through the dead leaves under the tree. What could be coming next! The scared, awkward owl turned his head over to one side and strained his big eyes to see. His ears stood up, and his pupils grew bigger and bigger with fright. He looked like a great booby entrapped by a practical joke. But this was too serious. What with a dozen vireos and thrushes threatening him, some wild animal or other rushing about at the foot of the tree, — and the pair of big glass eyes almost as large as his own, through which another mysterious object was menacing him. No owl could bear it! Away he flew, as fast as his blundering wings could flap, followed by the angry vireos, who saw him well

out of their neighborhood before they let him
alone.

The next day I scared up the foolish fellow
again, in the same place, and found that the nearest vireo's nest was gone! Not a trace was left,
nothing but one feather! Had he taken his re-
venge in the night? The trees refused to tell
tales, and I had to be satisfied with giving him
such a scare as would keep him away in future.

XXXVI.

YELLOW-THROATED VIREO.

THE name of this beautiful bird calls up college
days, for my first memory of him is a picture of
one of the fairest May mornings upon which a
Connecticut Valley sun ever rose.

Dandelions were just beginning to dot the tender grass, and the air was full of busy travellers
stopping on their northward journey to see the
beautiful old New England town that the bird-
voiced Jenny Lind christened the " paradise of
America." Eager for a sight of the strangers, I
hid myself under the spreading boughs of an old
apple-tree in the corner of an orchard and waited
to see what would come.

A purple finch was now gathering materials for
her nest where she had been coquetting with her
handsome lover not long before, and the catbird

who lived across the road by the bank of Mill
River had flown over to talk with the visitors;
while above the rest full and rich came the song
of the handsome rose-breasted grosbeak. My
cover was a happy thought. Right into the tree
over my head came the birds, so busy flitting
about the leaves they had little time to look under
the branches. And most beautiful of all — though
a rainbow of warblers came before I left — was
this dainty, golden-throated vireo.

Less restless than the warblers, he inspected the
boughs more thoroughly, giving me at intervals
glimpses of his olive back, white wing bars, and
bright yellow chin and throat as well as his pretty
yellow breast that turns to white below. *Whe-he-
he*, he sang out as he worked, and I suspect his
sharp eyes detected me when he turned his head
on one side and peered through the leaves.

How delighted I was to discover, a few weeks
later, that he or one of his brothers had gone to
housekeeping on the campus! The nest was the
first vireo basket I had ever seen, and I well remember the enthusiasm it excited in the other
college girls. We would go out after breakfast,
wade through the damp grass to the maple from
which it hung, and stand looking up at it, admiring the bits of white trimming fastened on at regular intervals along the sides, and exclaiming at
the beauty of the architect watching us from among
the leaves, until, at last, the tolling of the chapel
bell would send us hurrying back up the hill.

XXXVII.

WARBLING VIREO.

THE warbling is the smallest of the three vireos. Its back is grayish olive, and its breast is tinged with yellow. It may be distinguished from the others by his song.

Dr. Brewer says: "This vireo . . . is to a large extent a resident of villages, towns, and even cities. It is by far the sweetest singer that ventures within their crowded streets and public squares, . . . and the melody of its song is exquisitely soft and beautiful. It is chiefly to be found among the tall trees, in the vicinity of dwellings, where it seems to delight to stay, and from their highest tops to suspend its pensile nest. It is especially abundant among the elms on Boston Common."

By reason of their dainty coats and shapely forms, their pretty ways and their repose of manner, the vireos remind one most forcibly of the waxwings.

Birds naturally group themselves by occupation, and, as a Darwinian corollary, by coloring. The sparrows spend most of their time on the ground searching for seeds, and are protected by their earth-colored suits; the woodpeckers live clinging to tree trunks, and many of them are disguised by their likeness to the bark; the flycatchers take their living from the insects that swarm in the air, and their dull colors serve as non-conductors of attention; while the vireos, who live on measure-worms and similar morsels, are so exclusively devoted to foliage that they might well be called leaf-birds, and their tints harmonize strikingly with their habits. They may well be known as "greenlets."

XXXVIII.

OVEN-BIRD ; GOLDEN-CROWNED THRUSH.

WE have had the loud rattling trill of the yellow hammer, the alarm of the kingfisher, and the fine, shrill trill of the chipping sparrow, but now we come to one that differs from them all. Mr. Burroughs has aptly described it by the word *teach-er*. It seems to beat upon the air, growing louder and louder, increasing in intensity, volume, and rapidity until the end, like

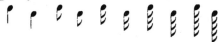

teach-er, teach-er, teach-er, teach-er, teacher

Ordinarily the trill is your clue in looking for the oven-bird. When you hear it close at hand, and fail to see him on a tree, look carefully under the bushes on the ground. If you see a bird the size of the white-throated sparrow, tossing the dead leaves aside with his bill and scratching them up, less like a chewink than like a hen, you have probably found your friend.

His olive-green back makes him inconspicuous when he is among the leaves, and the thick brown spotting on his white breast serves as a disguise when he is on the ground. If you are fortunate you will discover his orange-brown crown, enclosed by two black stripes that converge toward the bill.

Like the partridge, the crow, the blackbirds, and the meadow-lark, the oven-bird is a walker, so that you can distinguish him at a glance merely by his leisurely dignified gait, — it is such a contrast to the hopping of the chewinks and sparrows.

The leaf-house from which the oven-bird gets his name varies in its roofing, but the first nest I ever found may be taken as a type of the commonest style of architecture. It was a bright morning in June, and while walking through the edge of a grove of young maples a brown shadow started up from under my feet and disappeared in the woods. On looking down beside a blooming Solomon's seal, I saw what at first glance seemed to be a bunch of dry leaves, — one of the thousand pushed up by mice or crowding spring flowers. But the hint given by the fleeting shadow could not be ignored, and I stooped down to examine the bunch. I felt it over eagerly, — one, two, three sides, no opening; the fourth, my fingers slipped in, — it was the unique oven-bird's nest I had been hoping to find ever since I was a child.

In an instant I was on hands and knees peering through the mysterious doorway. How interesting! There lay five exquisite eggs, their irregular brown speckles centring in a crown about the larger end. What a wonderful builder the little creature seemed! His arched roof was lined so smoothly with soft dry leaves it suggested a fretwork ceiling. What a tiny palace of beauty had this golden-crowned queen of the thrushes! What mystery that bunch of leaves held! The little brown lady might have been sitting at the mouth of a fairy cave.

The next day I found three of the eggs hatched, and such absurd-looking nestlings had well been taken for bird gnomes. They seemed all mouth and eyeball! Small red appendages answered for wings, and tufts of gray down on the skin did for a coat of feathers. Even when feebly throwing up their heads and opening their big yellow throats for worms, the birds' eyes were closed so fast they had an uncanny appearance. The same day I had the good fortune to stumble upon another nest. This was essentially the same, though built more of fine roots.

The ingenuity of the builders is shown by a device which puzzled me greatly in my first nest. I made several visits to it, and when the little ones had flown, found that the grass around the

mouth of the nest had been pulled together, so as
to leave only a round hole just large enough for
the bird to go in and out. For some time I was
at a loss to account for it, but I had noticed from
the outset that this bird acted peculiarly. On

none of my visits had she uttered a note or come
near me, while the other mother oven-birds always
began smacking their bills and flying hither and
thither the instant I appeared. Perhaps this
mother was more thoughtful than the others, and
considering their clatter dangerous, went to the
other extreme.

The most terrified oven-bird that I have ever
seen I found on a densely wooded hillside in the
same woods. She began her smacking as soon as
we came in sight, but although we hunted carefully for the nest we could not find a trace of it.
We sat down on a log and waited for her to show

it to us, but that did no good. She did confine herself to a radius of about three rods, but selecting saplings at extreme points flew from one to the other as she inspected us, all the while wagging her tail nervously up and down and keeping up the monotonous smacking.

Finding her as incorrigible as the mosquitoes, and realizing the approach of the dinner hour, my friend and I set out for home. But in our case the gods favored the cowardly, for, as we were brandishing our maple twigs in the faces of pursuing punkies and mosquitoes, we suddenly started up the little family we had been hunting for.

They ran out from the leaves under our feet, scudding off in all directions. My two dogs pounced after them, and we flew in terror after the dogs, but Balder's big jaws had nearly engulfed them before we had dragged him off. In the midst of the confusion the terrified mother flew to the ground and began trailing in a pitifully excited way. She spread out her wings and tail, dragging them along the earth as if helpless. On finding that we would not accept that decoy, and seeing that her little ones had hidden away under the leaves, she tried another plan and walked once slowly back and forth for about a rod on the side away from her young. Having, as she supposed, completely diverted our attention by these imaginative ruses, as the dogs were perfectly quiet, and we had not moved since the first alarm, she made a detour and risked an examination of the place where the little birds had disappeared.

In watching the oven-bird I have been surprised to find how irregular individuals are in their time of nesting. On June 11 I found a family of full-grown young being fed in the branches of a maple-tree. The same day I found a nest full of eggs. June 12 three of these eggs hatched, and I found a nest of young a quarter grown. June 13 I found the family that I have just described well out of their nest. These could hardly have been first and second broods, as they were in all stages of development. This same difference I have since found in the nesting of robins, vireos, chipping birds, song sparrows and others.

When I considered myself well acquainted with the oven-bird and its notes, I was much surprised to be told that it had a beautiful song distinct from the usual trill. The trill seems to be used for all its commonplace thoughts and feelings, but, as Mr. Bicknell says, "on occasion, as if sudden emotion carried it beyond the restrictions that ordinarily beset its expression, it bursts forth with a wild outpouring of intricate and melodious song. This song is produced on the wing, oftenest when the spell of evening is coming over the woods. Sometimes it may be heard as an outburst of vesper melody carried above the foliage of the shadowy forest and descending and dying away with the waning twilight."

Mr. Bicknell speaks only of the two songs, but I have heard the two combined. The outbreak of high, rapid, confused notes being interlarded with the low-pitched conversational trilling *teach'-er, teach'er*. By increasing the confusion, this adds greatly to the effect of excitement spoken of by Mr. Bicknell. Though most common at evening or in the night, I have frequently heard this medley in both morning and afternoon. The rhythm and volume of this interesting song in its simplest form may be suggested by the syllables *whee'he, whee'he, whee'ha, he' he' ha*, increasing in volume toward the middle, and unlike the ordinary trill, diminishing in intensity again at the close.

XXXIX.

JUNCO; SLATE-COLORED SNOWBIRD.

EARLY in September you may have found the juncos, companies of little gray-robed monks and nuns, just emerging from the forests where they cloister during the summer months. Most of them nest well to the north, but still there are many that content themselves with the cool mountain ranges of the Alleghanies.

If they build in your locality, as they do here, their habits, like those of the chickadee, are greatly changed in summer, and you will take more than one casual walk through the woods before you discover them. They are no longer in flocks, but in pairs, and I consider myself fortunate if I get a timid look from one from among the dead branches of a fallen tree top.

Early last May I was delighted to see a pair on the edge of the raspberry patch, but though they inspected the recesses of a pile of brush, seemed greatly interested in the nooks and crannies of an upturned root, and reviewed the attractions of a pretty young hemlock that stood in a moss-grown swamp on the border of the patch, I suspect it was only a feint; and when they came to the grave business of house choosing they followed family traditions and built under a stump, in a hole beneath the root of a tree, under an overhanging bank, or somewhere else on the ground, with a natural roof to keep off the rain.

At all events, they left the raspberry patch, and with the exception of one or two that I heard giving their high-keyed woodsy trill in June, that was the last time I saw any of the family there until fall. Then they came out in time to meet their cousins the white-throats, and stayed till after the first snows.

Like the sparrows, waxwings, blackbirds, swallows, blue jays, swifts, and others, the juncos live in flocks when not nesting. One day in September I found a number of them gathered around an old barn, some sitting quietly on the boards and sticks that lay on the ground, and others, as

becomes inhabitants of No. 4, hopping about picking up seeds.

Another day they and some white-throats were
by the side of the barn eating grain scattered at
the threshing. Not content with what they could
find there, some of them flew up on the sill of a
small window, hopped along, and actually disappeared in the dark barn.

As the weather grew colder they came, as they
do every spring and fall, to see what they could
find to eat by the side of the house. Here, where
they find only friends, they raise their heads with
quiet curiosity when you approach, and seem
notably gentle, trustful birds; but it is said that
they show much caution as well as intelligence in
eluding their enemies, and are among the most
difficult birds to snare.

XL.

KINGLETS.

Do you know these dainty little birds that visit
us twice a year? Some bright September morning you wake up and find them flitting about the
apple-trees, and know that fall has come. But
they tell you the fact in such a breezy, cheery way
that you remember only how glad you are to see
them. In April they are back just long enough
to sing out " How do you do ? " and then are off
for the north so that summer shan't catch them.

How do they look ? Well, they are fluffy little
things with grayish olive coats and whitish vests
that protect them as they flit about the leaves as
perfectly as the vireo's suits. That is the way I
thought of them when I had only a vague idea
that one of the family had a golden crest, and the
other wore a ruby crown. But one fall, when
they came back to the old thorn-apple by the
garden, I thought I would learn to know the
cousins apart.

That morning one little fellow had the tree all
to himself. And what a queer gnome he was! A
fat ball of feathers, stilted up on long, wiry legs,
with eyes that, though set oddly enough far back
from his bill, were yet so near together they seemed
to prevent his seeing straight ahead. He would
flash one eye on me, and then jerk himself round
and flash the other, scolding in the funniest way
with his fine chatter. I could not see that he had
any crown at all, and so was as much puzzled as
ever to decide which kinglet he was.

He and his friends were here by themselves
about two weeks, working industriously all the
while — dear little brownies — to clear our mountain ashes and apple-trees of insects before leaving
us. I came to know them as far off as I could
see them by their restless bluebird way of lifting
their wings and twinkling them in the air as they
hunted through the branches. And how they did
hunt! As the kinglets live among the leaves,

they adopt the tints of the vireos, though they are
as little like them as the fluffy chickadee is like
the waxwing in build or temperament. The vireos
walk sedately down the length of a branch, calmly
turning their heads on one side to peer under the
leaves for their measure-worm; but the kinglets!
— clambering up a limb, turning from one side
to the other, with one big eye always close to the
bark staring for insects; fluttering under a twig
like a humming-bird, and then catching hold upside down to pick off an insect; flitting about
from branch to branch; stopping a moment to
eye me inquisitively, and then hurrying on with
their work — the restless pigmies seemed most
unvireo like.

At the end of two weeks I had seen no kinglet
crown of any kind. But one day I had a surprise.
Hearing a faint note from a Norway spruce I
looked up and saw a kinglet, but — what was it?
Instead of being one of my gnomes, he was the
most human, every-day sort of a bird, with a
naïve interrogative air that might have argued
him an American. Then his tiny, stubby bill
stuck out from his big head with such a pert,
business-like air it gave my idea of kinglets another shock. What was he? Could I have been
wholly mistaken? Was my elf no kinglet at all
— was *this* the kinglet? Such a crown! I had
comforted myself for my gnome's lack of crown
by thinking that it was concealed like the king-

bird's, but here, — how could such a crown as this
ever have been hidden? Why, the black lines
came way down to his absurd little bill, and the
gold between them was plain enough to be seen
almost as far off as the bird himself.

I came in bewildered enough, but the moment
I saw DeKay's plates I understood it all. This
was the golden-crowned, and my pigmies were the
ruby-crowned kinglets. After that the two kinds
were here in great numbers for two weeks, and
before the rubies left I surprised one of them into
showing his beautiful scarlet crown. The ruby-
crowns went as they had come, two weeks in advance of the goldens.

When they were both here I used to stand
under the apple-trees and watch them. Sometimes there must have been twenty in one tree.
They were very tame, but rarely found time to
look at me.

Seen together the golden is appreciably the
smaller; his legs look shorter, and he is not so
plump, — appears more like an ordinary bird.
His back is grayer than the ruby's, and when his
wings are crossed over it you get an effect of bars
near the tips. Mr. Golden-crown has a concealed
patch of cadmium orange in the centre of his
crown, but his wife is content with the plain gold,
and the children often show neither black nor
gold. The goldens seem to have less of the wild
bluebird habit of lifting their wings when lit, but

they hang upside down even more than the rubies, often flying up from one spray to light upside down on the one above. The goldens have a business-like way of getting under a leaf and picking off the insects one after another as fast as their tiny bills can work. Their song is said to be inferior to that of the rubies, which is considered a ten-days' marvel coming from such a tiny bird.

XLI.

SNOW BUNTING ; SNOWFLAKE.

This is the true snowbird, and though it belongs in the same pigeon-hole — that of the finches and sparrows — it can never be confounded with the junco. The monastic juncos are closely shrouded in slate-gray robes and cowls, only a short under robe of white being marked off below their breasts. The snowflakes, on the other hand, as their name suggests, are mostly white, although their backs are streaked with dusky and black.

The juncos come about the house in spring and fall, and during the early snows, but the snowbirds, timid and strange, fly over the fields and are associated with the wonderful white days of a country winter, when the sky is white, the earth is white, and the white trees bow silently under the wand of winter till they stand an enchanted snow forest. For, as the flakes drift through the

air, the snowbirds, undulating between the white
earth and sky, seem like wandering spirits that
are a part of the all-pervading whiteness. Thoreau says, " they are the true spirits of the snowstorm. They are the animated beings that ride
upon it and have their life in it."

Mr. Allen, in speaking of our winter birds,
says : " The beautiful snow buntings when whirling from field to field in compact flocks, their
white wings glistening in the sunlight, form one
of the most attractive sights of winter." He adds
that they are the " bad weather birds " of the su-
perstitious, as they usually appear mysteriously
during snowstorms and disappear in the weeks
of fine weather. He says : " Cold, half-arctic
countries being their chosen home, they only
favor us with their presence during those short
intervals when their food in the northern fields
is too deeply buried ; and being strong of wing
and exceedingly rapid in flight, they can in a few
hours leave the plain for the mountain, or migrate
hundreds of miles to the northward."

Late in December I have seen a flock of them
flying over the meadows with the rhythmical undulating motion of their cousins the goldfinches,
twittering *ter-ra-lee, ter-ra-lee, ter-ra-lee* as they
went. Now and then they would light for a moment to pick at the seeds appearing above the
snow, but soon they swept on toward the north.

XLII.

SCARLET TANAGER.

LIKE the vireos, the scarlet tanager is associated with green tree tops; but if you ask just where you will see him, it is hard to answer. In Northampton, I remember finding him in three quite dissimilar spots.

The bird of Paradise has become a familiar sight in our museums, but the good people of Northampton follow Dante and see "Paradise" itself before they die. "Purgatory" is there, too, for warning, and the river runs between the two abodes! They lie just outside the town, and if you could get some kindly spirit to guide you, they would surely seem well named.

"Purgatory" lies barren and desolate, strewn with sand and stones on which the sun beats down as if with intent to torture imprisoned souls. Opposite stands "Paradise," a wood of wondrous beauty, — a true elysium for the immortal spirits of birds and flowers! In its heart is a grove of musical pines, whose brown, pine-needle carpet is garlanded with clumps of ferns. Close to the river's edge, reaching their branches low over it as it narrows to a stream, the maples and birches offer cool green shade when the sun is parching the banks of "Purgatory"; and in autumn, when the bare sand and stones grow cold, the leaves of "Paradise" burn with the tints of sunset.

On the desolate margin of "Purgatory" you rarely see a human face, unless that of some poor soul-tormented lunatic who has strayed from the asylum on the hill. But in "Paradise" you meet groups of merry children, college girls gathering wild flowers, and all the town in gala-day attire.

This is the haunt of the birds, and here the Smith Audubon Society has gathered about Mr. Burroughs, listening to his interpretation of the chippering of the swifts that circle far overhead; hearkening with him to the yellow hammer's cries, and watching the happy goldfinches, busy in the button-wood tops. Here each level has its bird — from the leaves, the oven-bird sends up his crescendo; from among the bushes comes the quarrying note of the white-throats; low on the boughs of the trees the thrushes sit wrapt in meditation; in the top of a sapling the indigo-bird sings of the white violets beneath him; from the hemlocks and pines come the screams of the blue jays; over the river the kingfisher flies, sounding his alarm on the wing; and high overhead the soaring hawk circles in silence.

One spring morning when we were in one of the most beautiful spots of all Paradise, where a tiny rill spreads out over the sand, bathing the roots of the bright green grass and the blue forget-me-nots, a true bird of Paradise came flying over our heads, and uttering a loud *chuck ah,* hid away in the leaves. It was the *scarlet* tanager, the bird of glowing coal, whose brilliancy passes wonder. His black wings and tail seemed only to intensify his flaming coat, which literally dazzled my eyes as I looked at him. Little marvel that he takes pleasure in the green leaves! and chooses a wife — in most " *natural* selection " — who is also his complemental color!

But how could Madam Tanager ever live with such a fiery husband if her eyes did not find relief in her own greens? Even then it would seem that she had to become accustomed to him by degrees, for in his youth her gay cavalier is relieved by green, yellow, and black. Perhaps even his own eyes get tired, for like the bobolink and goldfinch in the fall he gets out his old clothes and flies away south in as plain a garb as his lady's.

Strolling through Paradise on another day I heard a song that I did not know, and leaving the river edge with its green grass and forget-me-nots, and clambering up the steep hillside where the magic witch-hazel blooms and shoots its seeds afar, I made my way cautiously to the tree from which the voice came. There, high over my head, was another scarlet tanager. He was evidently a young gentleman, for there was still a yellowish streak across his breast, but he sang his woodsy song with all the gusto of an old bass. It is loud and harsh, but in a rhythm that, as it has been pertinently expressed, suggests the swinging of a pendulum. *Kreé — kreé — ee — kreé — eah kreé — kreé — ee kreé — eah* back and forth, swinging a little further each time, the whole song often ending with an emphatic *chip' chirr.*

The third place where I found the tanager in Northampton — and this seemed to be more of a true haunt — was at Fort Hill on the south of the town, where, across the meadows, Mount Holyoke and Mount Tom tower majestically. Here, on a sunny eastern hillside that looks away toward the Connecticut, the early adder tongues and hepaticas are found, and the scarlet tanager shows a friendliness that becomes the beautiful spot. Close to the footpath I have stood and watched him without exciting the least suspicion or fear.

Here at home I have seen one of the tanagers in an ash that shades the house, and they sing in various parts of our woods. Still, I feel most sure of finding them in a swamp back of the raspberry patch. While a botanical friend has been looking for rare orchids among the moss and ferns, I have followed one of the handsome birds through the length of the swamp, punctuating his song with broken bird talk. At times, as I stood on an old moss-covered log, he would come almost up to me, and then, just as I was admiring his flaming coat, would fly back singing to himself the loud swinging song that seemed to catch new beauty from the rich, cool verdure of the swamp.

Like the vireos, although the tanagers seem to prefer the higher branches and tree tops in singing and hunting, their nest, a "saucer shaped structure," constructed of wiry dead grass-stems and like materials, "is built usually on a low branch. The eggs are pale bluish or greenish, spotted or speckled with brown."

The tanagers belong in pigeon-hole No. 5, which is marked "tanagers," and is between the "finches, sparrows, etc.," of No. 4 and the swallows of No. 6. Unlike the flycatchers and sparrows the males are brilliant birds, whose plumage varies greatly with the season, and whose plain wives are in marked contrast to them. But compare their unobtrusive ways with those of the catbird, the restless kinglets, chickadees, and blue jays; and their habits with those of the ground-loving ovenbird, the nuthatch, snowbird, and partridge, and you will see that the difference lies deeper than color.

XLIII.

BROWN THRASHER.

In a Massachusetts sand flat, where nothing but sand burrs and low scrubby bushes could flourish, I heard my first thrasher song. There were a pair of birds in a clump of bushes, and we came up within a few yards without disturbing them. Their backs were rich reddish-brown, and their breasts creamy or "buffy white," spotted with brown, while their sides were heavily streaked.

The thrashers are about the length and build of the cuckoos, and before I had seen them near by I confused the two. But you can distinguish between them even at a distance, for the breast of the cuckoos is pure white, while that of the thrashers is heavily spotted. When you are near enough to discern shades, you see that the rich reddish-brown back of the thrasher is in strong contrast to the dull grayish-brown of the cuckoo. While the cuckoo is practically songless, the song of the thrasher is excelled by few of our birds, combining the flexibility of the catbird with the sweetness of the thrush.

The thrasher is said to show much intelligence in choosing the position for its nest. In dry sandy regions it seems to prefer the ground, but if the soil is damp or clayey it builds in bushes; and along river banks in the west, where sudden freshets would swamp a low nest, with notable foresight it secures its nest in trees, sometimes as high as fifteen or twenty feet from the ground.

During migration, last fall, I was looking for warblers in the raspberry patch one morning before breakfast. When near the edge of the woods I heard the suppressed *shreea* a gray squirrel makes when scolding between its teeth. It was so near that I looked down hoping to catch sight of the impudent bright eyes, but not a squirrel

could I see. A flock of warblers came just then
to take my attention, and it was some time before
I got across the patch. When I did, what was
my surprise and delight to find a brown thrasher
sitting near the ground on a drooping bass-wood
branch in the midst of a noisy company of white-
throats. He had evidently seen me, for his long
tail was perked up, his short wings hung at his
sides, and he looked up half appealingly, as much
as to say: "Oh dear, what did you come here
for? — I wish you would n't hurt me! — I suppose I 'd better hide," and so he hopped off to
another branch, looked back, saw me still staring,
and disappeared.

After breakfast I came back to the spot. Listening closely I heard the squirrel-like scold that
I had noticed before on the opposite side of the
patch, and something moving on the leaves under
the bushes by my side. What was this mysterious
creature ? Silently I turned toward it and gazed
through my glass, almost holding my breath to
hear. Again came the noise, and, between the
leaves, every few seconds I could catch sight of a
brown tail wagging up and down. Suddenly,
there it stood in full view, the thrasher ! I could
see even his yellow eyes ! He was only three or
four feet away, but hopped about quite unconcernedly until I made myself too conspicuous;
then he vanished, and I hunted the patch over for
another glimpse of him. When I did find him,

he was sitting quietly on the top of a small stump. He had no objection to make to me then, but when Balder began stalking around among the bushes he stretched up till he made himself look comically like a long narrow-necked bottle, when he took a survey and departed.

XLIV.

ROSE-BREASTED GROSBEAK.

JUST back of the Smith College campus, on the bank of Mill River, where the catbird talked to himself in the sunny orchard, the handsome purple finch made love to his lady bird, and the cuckoo hid away among the leaves, the rose-breasted grosbeak used to stop before beginning housekeeping. A big maple in one corner of the orchard by the river was his favorite cover, but we have watched him sing quite fearlessly in a small elm on the outside of the orchard, close to the road.

What a beauty he was too! He wore a decorous glossy black coat and white vest, but where his black choker touched his shirt front — was it a beautiful pink rose he had fastened on to catch the eye of his lady? And as he flew past, showing white blotches on his tail and at its base, was that rose powder with which he had touched the under side of his wings? His wife was as good a foil to him as her cousins, the plain little purple finch and indigo-bird are to their handsome husbands. She looked decidedly like a sparrow, and had patches of saffron-yellow under her wings, where the male had carmine. Both had heavy finch bills. His was yellow, and he scraped it on the side of a branch as a man would sharpen a knife on a whetstone — first on one side and then on the other. Perhaps we should say, men sharpen their knives as birds do their bills, for it is more likely that the birds set the fashion!

The song of the grosbeak is loud, clear, and sweet, with a rhythm like the tanager's. It is a longer song, however, with the rough edges rounded off, and has, moreover, something of the oriole quality. The call note is as characteristic as the *chip chirr* of the tanager. It is a thin, unsteady *kick*, and usually prefaces the song.

The nest of the grosbeak in " Paradise " was in the border of a thicket, almost within our reach, and when we discovered it, Mr. Grosbeak's big black head and yellow bill were protruding over the edge. We could not help laughing at this domestic turn, he looked so out of place; but we liked him all the better for minding the babies while his wife took a rest.

XLV.

WHIPPOORWILL.

In the warm summer twilight as we drive along
the bank of Black River, watching the sunset
glow fade in the west, and catching its glistening
reflection in the water, over the low foot-hills of
the Adirondacks on the east comes the big red
harvest moon. Then, as we stop the horses to
listen, even the sibilant whirr of the locusts'
wings and the subdued chirring of the crickets
are hushed, for out of the woods comes the loud
wild call — *whip-poor-will, whip-poor-will, whip-
poor-will.*

The whippoorwill belongs to the family of
"goatsuckers, swifts, etc.," and so must be put
in the drawer where the chimney swift, humming-
bird, partridge, cuckoos, woodpeckers, and all the
others that did not belong to the order of "perching birds" were left by themselves.

XLVI.

WINTER WREN.

One October day when the raspberry patch
was astir with fluttering kinglets and warblers,
and noisy with the quarrying of white-throats,
and the muttered excuses and *wait, wait* of tardy

crows flying hurriedly over to the caucus in the
next woods, I found the piquant little winter
wrens bobbing about among the bushes oblivious
to everything but their own particular business.

I gave one of them a start as I came on him
unexpectedly, and so, on catching sight of a second, kept cautiously quiet. But, if you please,
as soon as he got a glimpse of me, the inquisitive
brown sprite came hurrying from one raspberry
stem to another, with his absurd bit of a square
tail over his back, and never once stopped till he
got near enough for a good look. There he clung,
atilt of a stem, bobbing his plump little body
from side to side, half apologetically, but saying
quip with an air that assured me he was afraid of
no giants, however big! When I had admired
his mottled, dusky vest and his rusty brown coat
with its fine dusky barring, and noted the light
line over his eye, and the white edging of his
wing ; and when he had decided to his satisfaction what I was doing there in the woods, he went
hopping along, under an arching fern, off to the
nearest stump.

When they are out hunting, their tails standing
over their backs, their necks bent forward and
their straight bills sticking out ahead, these little
wrens have a most determined air! First you
see one examining the sides and top of an old
stump, running about, dipping down into the hollow, and then flitting off among the bushes, chat-

tering *quip-quap* as he goes. Then one flies
against the side of a tree to peck at a promising
bit of bark and clambers several feet up the
trunk to show what a good gymnast he is ; and
finally one pops up with a worm in his mouth,
shakes it well before eating, and afterwards wipes
his bill with the energy characteristic of the active, healthy temper of the whole wren family.

On the twelfth of October the ground was covered with snow, and the woods were so white and
still I hardly expected to find anything in the
raspberry patch. But walking through I discovered one of the little wrens, as active and busy as
ever. As I stood watching him he climbed into
the cosiest cover of leaves that a bush ever offered
a bird for shelter, and I supposed he would settle
himself to wait for the sun. But no ! he examined it carefully, turning his head on one side
and then the other, probably thinking it would
be a very nice place for some tender worm, and
then flew out into the cold snowy bushes again.

On the twenty-second of the month, when we
had had a still heavier fall of snow, and the
wrens found it too cold even to take dinner from
a golden-rod stem, one of the confiding little birds
came to hunt on the piazza right in front of my
study window. You should have seen him work !
He ignored the crumbs I threw out for him, but
flitted about, running over the shrivelled vines
trained over the piazza, and examining all the

cracks and crannies where a fly might edge itself into the moulding. Once he dropped a worm, and you should have seen him come tumbling down after it!

The nest of this brave little bird is snug and warm, made of moss, lined with soft feathers, and lodged " in crevices of dead logs or stumps in thick, coniferous woods." What a pleasure it would be to follow him north, and study all his pretty ways in the dark forest home, where he furnishes mirth and sunshine all the summer through.

The wren is found in pigeon-hole No. 10, along with his cousins the thrasher and catbird. "Wrens, thrashers, etc.," is on the door-plate — perhaps the catbird is left out because he always takes pains to announce himself. All the household have long bills, and the catbird and thrasher have also long tails, with very short wings ; while they all have a piquant way of perking up their tails when startled.

In contrast to the vireos, tanagers, and orioles, these birds spend most of their time in shrubs or bushes rather than in high trees. Different birds take various levels — stories in their out-of-doors house. The sparrows and chewinks live in the basement — on the ground-floor; the wrens and thrashers on the first floor in bushes and shrubs ; the indigo-bird on the third floor — low trees ; the vireos and tanagers and orioles on the fourth floor — high trees ; while the swallows and swifts go above all — in the air.

XLVII.

RED-HEADED WOODPECKER.

THE handsome red-head can be distinguished at almost any distance by his sharply blocked "tricolor" of glossy blue-black, bright crimson, and clear white. Beginning with his red head, the stripes of the French flag are reversed, for the order is not red, white, and blue, but red, blue (black), and white. Underneath he is pure white. Mr. Burroughs speaks of his flitting about the open woods, "connecting the trees by a gentle arc of crimson and white!"

When common, the red-headed woodpecker may be found everywhere, — in the orchards, gardens, fields, and woods, — but in many parts of the country he is rather rare. He is an erratic migrant, his residence in any district depending on the nut supply ; so that you may not see him for a year or more at a time.

Like the California woodpecker, the red-heads are "hoarders." They have been found making a business of storing away beech nuts. They would hide them not only in knot-holes, between cracks in the bark, and under strips of loosened bark, but also in fence posts, railroad ties, and

between shingles on the roofs of houses; and in
several instances when their store-house was full,
the woodpeckers would take the precaution to
roof it over with a layer of empty hulls, or bits
of wood and bark.

XLVIII.

YELLOW-BELLIED SAPSUCKER.

In the spring the yellow-bellied woodpecker is
a mercurial Frenchman compared with the sober,
self-contained Englishmen, his cousins, the hairy
and downy. They contrast as scarlet and gray.
Even their dress marks them. The hairy and
downy are robed like grave philosophers in black
and white, the old fathers merely donning a red
cap for dignity. But though the sapsucker has
to be content with a mottled black and white coat,
besides a red cap, he wears a crimson frontlet, a
bib-shaped piece of crimson satin fastened close
under his chin, and bordering this a circlet of
black satin, below which, and falling to his feet,
is his pale yellow robe.

In April and May, especially during courting,
the air is full of his boisterous cries. In the edge
of the woods, in the orchard, by the side of the
house, the excited birds flicker from tree to tree,
chasing each other about. Sometimes two of
them march up opposite sides of the same tree,

with arching necks and rapid, taunting cries of
chuck'ah, chuck'ah, chuck'ah, chuck'ah, and then
circle around the trunk after each other like a
pair of hot-headed suitors quarrelling over their
lady-love. When they are in a calmer mood their
cry, though still emphatic, loses much of its taunting tone, and is more like *che whee', che whee',
che whee', che whee'.* They have a variety of call
notes, such as *kree, kray; yah', yah',* and *kre' ah,*
all full of spirited emphasis. But their ebullient
feelings cannot be expressed in that way; they
must needs take to drumming and *tinning.* I
quote from an account of their performances published ten years ago by my brother, Dr. C. Hart
Merriam. It is interesting to note that their
habits have not changed in that time. He says:
" At this season scarcely an hour passes from
daylight to sunset that one or more cannot be
heard drumming with commendable perseverance
upon the tin-roofs, eave-troughs, or escape-pipes
of our house or some of the out-buildings. They
strike the tin violently half a dozen or more times,
evidently enjoying the sound thus produced, and
then rest a few minutes before repeating the performance. Each woodpecker usually returns to
the same spot, and on our roof are several patches
the size of one's hand, from which the paint has
been entirely drummed off. On the escape-pipe
they sometimes follow around a joint, and by con-
stant and long-continued pounding so loosen the

solder that the dependent portion of the pipe falls
down. How they manage to cling to these vertical pipes and the nearly perpendicular portions of
the roof is a mystery. I have seen both sexes
at work on our roof, but the female does not
often indulge in this pastime, and is rarely observed to take part in the boisterous gambols
of the males. In the groves and forests where
tin-roofed buildings do not abound, the yellow-
bellied woodpeckers amuse themselves by pounding upon such dry hollow trees and hard resonant
limbs as multiply the sound tenfold, so that one
can at a distance readily distinguish them from
other members of the family."

The name "sapsucker" is more appropriately
applied to the yellow-bellied woodpecker than to
the nuthatch, for instead of taking an occasional
taste of the sap at the sugar-bush in spring, he
spends much of his time riddling live trees with
squarish holes, to which he returns to drink the
oozing sap and feast upon the insects that gather.

The woodpeckers, I have noticed, all work in
about the same way, varying their methods to suit
the character of the wood. The only time I ever
watched the sapsucker drill a maple he worked
like the hairy, first giving a dozen or more quick
blows with his head turned on one side, and then
as many more with his head on the other side —
just as a carpenter chisels, cutting out a wedge
instead of going straight down. After working

in this way for a time, he seemed to pick out bits of wood — his shavings — and drop them to the ground. When tired working at one hole he would go on to another. The bark was torn from an area of several inches, and this was riddled with holes apparently in process of making. The woodpeckers are not perching birds, and so must be put in the drawer with the kingfisher, cuckoo, humming-birds, and others. Of the five we have had, the yellow hammer is the least of a woodpecker, building comparatively low, having a trill that takes the place of a song, hunting on the ground and fences as well as on trees for his food, and, accordingly, assuming an earth-colored disguise that would be of little use to the other woodpeckers. The sapsucker and the yellow hammer go south for the winter, but the downy and hairy are permanent residents, while the red-headed woodpecker's presence is entirely dependent on the food supply. The sapsucker is the most boisterous of the five — the sombre hairy and downy the most silent. Of them all the redhead is the family beauty.

XLIX.

GREAT-CRESTED FLYCATCHER.

In spring, when a loud piercing whistle comes shrilling from the woods —one note given in rising inflection — I know that the great-crested fly-catcher has arrived. There is always an excite-ment about the event that prompts you to seize your hat and rush out to find him. And a sight of him up in a tree top is worth more than one walk!

By the side of the other flycatchers in pigeon-hole No. 1, he stands at the head of the family. What an aristocratic bearing his great crest gives him! And look at his olive coat, his ash-gray vest, and his bright sulphur - yellow knickerbockers! You almost expect him to produce wig and shoe-buckles! Then compare his manners with those of his plain gray cousins. Do you suppose he could let his wings and his fine rufous tail hang down as the least flycatcher, the phœbe, and the wood pewee do? And could such a dignified bird demean himself with the petty bickerings of the kingbird, or the recklessness of the warlike least flycatcher?

The great-crest flies restlessly among the tree tops, uttering his shrill cry, and soliloquizing in a low warbling twitter. He also has a loud short chatter reserved for occasion, and I have seen him on a tree by the house scolding away with a *whee ree.*

His nest shows all the eccentricity of genius. It is usually made in a knot - hole, at varying heights from the ground. But the strangest thing about it, and that which distinguishes it from the nests of all other North American birds, is the remarkable fact that cast-off snake skins are used in its construction. This is true even in localities where snakes are so uncommon that an ordinary person may spend a lifetime without finding one of their skins. Surely the birds must possess keen eyes and much local knowledge of the haunts of the snakes when the shedding process is going on!

Mrs. Treat tells of a pair of great-crested fly-catchers that built in a bird-house on top of the stable. First, she says, they go to all the bird-houses " scattered about on the posts " in the vineyard, but as we would expect of such aristo-crats, choose " the finest establishment on the premises — a three-storied, octagon house, sur-mounted with a cupola and spire, with a weather vane and ball attached." Though a pair of blue-birds have kept all would-be tenants away for several years, they offer no resistance to the fly-catchers, who settle in the empty cupola.

L.

BANK SWALLOW; SAND MARTIN.

LIKE the kingfisher the bank swallow excavates a hole for his nest, and when you are driving through cuts in sand or clay banks you will often see the birds pop out of their holes in the sides and fly off up in the air. They are the plainest of our common swallows, being dead grayish-brown above and white below, with a band of grayish-brown across the breast, so that vanity does not interfere with their underground life.

LI.

EAVE SWALLOW; CLIFF SWALLOW.

THE cliff swallow is the common swallow that we constantly see on telegraph wires and about barns in company with the barn swallow. It is easy enough to distinguish between them, because the tail of the eave, instead of being deeply forked, is almost square; its back, instead of being glossy steel-blue, is dull blackish, and it also lacks the steel-blue collar.

The nest of the cliff swallow is "a gourd or retort-shaped structure composed of pellets of mud mixed with a few straws and lined with soft feathers, attached to the face of overhanging cliffs or underneath the eaves of buildings."

LII.

CROSSBILLS.

IN November, 1887, one of the commonest sounds heard on my walks was an odd metallic *kimp, kimp, kimp,* coming from a flock of crossbills far up in the air. They were often so high that I could not see them, and one day several flocks passed over my head, affording only a glimpse of black dots for them all. Their note often came from the hemlocks back in the woods, and on Thanksgiving morning I had the satisfaction of seeing the noisy strangers.

They had come out in the clearing, and lighted near a milk-house, some on a tree and others on the ground. I crept up as noiselessly as the crusty snow would allow, and, screening myself behind another building, watched them for some time. They seemed nervous, for every few minutes they started up simultaneously with a whirr, flew about a few seconds, and then settled down again.

When they were resting, those that were not chattering warbled to themselves in a sweet undertone, but when a new company joined their ranks they all began jabbering, and it was a grave question if any of them could hear what they were asking, or their neighbors trying to tell. Then as they broke up into groups and went wheeling about in the air, the glittering gilt deer weathervane on top of a barn a few rods away attracted them, and some of them lit on the horns a moment in passing. Several squads of them flew away, and as the confusion decreased the others grew less restless, and twenty or thirty flew down under the milk-house door and began picking up what they could find on the stones.

Such a mixture of colors! The old gentlemen were the handsomest, being some shade of red, while their wives and children were olivaceous or grayish. They seemed like a shifting kaleidoscope of colors, as they hopped about busily hunting for food.

Among them were a few of their cousins, the pine finches, and I thought I heard some goldfinches with those that passed over. I got the pretty visitors a basket of grain, and scattered it on the crust for them, but they seemed to prefer cone seeds, for they soon flew over to the spruces.

Unmindful of the laws of adaptation of which these bills are such an interesting example, the legend accounts for them in its own beautiful way. It has it that the birds tried to pull the nails from the cross, and in doing so twisted their bills in such a way that wherever they go they will always bear the symbol of their merciful deed.

The crossbills are very erratic in habit, and wander over large areas where they do not remain to build. They nest throughout the coniferous forests of the northern United States and Canada, and in mountains of the Southern States, notably in North Carolina, Tennessee, and Kentucky.

A curious example of this bird's fondness for salt is recorded by Mr. Romeyn B. Hough. An old ice-cream freezer, after becoming permeated with salt, was thrown out where the crossbills had access to it, and throughout the winter flocks of the birds came to it, like deer to a salt-lick. They were so eager that, in some places, they actually nibbled almost through the wood until, as Mr. Hough says, the freezer looked as if mice had been gnawing it.

LIII.

NIGHT-HAWK; BULL BAT.

Just at twilight, above the chippering of the chimney swifts, you will often hear sharp cries that startle you into looking overhead. Circling in the air after insects you will see large, dark colored birds, with narrow, clear cut, crescent shaped wings and slender bodies. If they come near enough you will catch the white bars on their wings as they fly rapidly by. If your eyes and glass are both good perhaps you will get a glimpse of their curious great mouths, wide open as they fly; and then the mysterious disappearance of the swarms of insects that hover in the air will be picturesquely explained.

A study of bills would be as suggestive as interesting. With each group, as we have seen, the form is modified to suit the needs of the birds, — the woodpeckers have long strong bills for hammering and excavating; the sparrows short stout cones for seed cracking; the vireos long slender bills for holding worms; and the flycatchers bills hooked at the end for holding insects; but perhaps the most extreme cases of adaptation are to be found in those of the kingfisher, humming-bird, crossbill, and night-hawk. In the night-hawk and whippoorwill the enormous fish-trap of

the kingfisher is exchanged for — almost no bill at all, merely a hook and eye for a wide gaping mouth.

The night-hawk and whippoorwill are the most nearly related of the four birds we have from the order of "goatsuckers, swifts, etc." They are both brown-mottled birds, and are similar in build and general habit. The swifts resemble the night-hawks in having narrow clear cut wings, small bills, and big mouths, but in habit they are almost

as unlike them as the humming-bird. All four
birds have strong wings, however, and so, as a
group, contrast with the sparrows in No. 4, and
the wrens and thrashers in No. 10.

LIV.

GRASS FINCH ; VESPER SPARROW ; BAY-WINGED BUNTING.

WHEN riding in the country it is well to carry
your opera-glass and examine the birds you find
on the fences along the road. Sparrows are very
common, and if you see one running along the
fence ahead of you, whose streaked back seems
too light for a song sparrow, you will do well to
watch him closely. When he flies up, if you see
white tail feathers, you know who your friend is
at once ; the meadow-lark and the grass finch are
two of the commonest of the few white tail-feath-
ered birds. His white breast and sides are streaked, and the markings on his back almost give the
effect of stripes. But the chestnut-brown on his
wings and his white tail feathers are enough to
distinguish him among the sparrows. His song
resembles that of the song sparrow, but while it
wants the cheery brightness we love in that, its
plaintive element gives it a richness which the
other lacks.

The grass finch is a timorous little bird, and his

interest in the genus *Homo* seems to be confined to the people who pass along the road. These appear to fascinate him, and it is always with reluctance that he flies away before them. A grass finch he certainly is. He nests in the grass, hops about in the grass, lives upon seeds he finds in the grass, and rarely gets much farther away than a roadside fence, or a tree that is surrounded by grass.

LV.

TREE SPARROW.

THE tree sparrows look much like their cousin chippy, but have something of the free mountain air and pine-tree atmosphere about them that the domestic chippy lacks.

I find them in spring and fall along the edge of the woods, or in the fields, eating grass seed; and a flock of them spent last April with us, singing with the fox sparrows in the evergreens, and coming about the house in the most friendly manner. Indeed the lordly little creatures quite took possession of the corn boxes in front of the dining-room window, and drove off the juncos with a sad show of temper. I forgave them, however, for I had a capital chance to observe them while they were eating the buckwheat.

Chippy, you know, has a way of crouching close to the ground. The tree sparrows, on the contrary, are erect, dignified looking birds, and raise their dark rufous caps with much more effect than chippy ever does. They differ from him, too, in having the lower part of their backs unstriped, in having rusty washings on the sides of their ashy breasts, and a dusky spot in the centre of the breast similar to the song sparrow's breastpin. Their song, though thinner than that of the song sparrow, is sweet and pleasing.

LVI.

WHITE-CROWNED SPARROW.

During migration the white-crowns generally keep by themselves, though sometimes they may be seen in flocks of white-throated sparrows, so it is well to inspect each bird carefully. The crown will enable you to discriminate between them, for in the white-crown the marking gives more the effect of a soldier's cap, the bands of clear white encircling the back of the head. This adds to the distinguished air of the bird, which, with his clearer grays and browns, his more shapely figure and erect carriage, soon become enough to mark him in themselves. For, as the great-crested fly-catcher overshadows the plebeian phœbe, the white-crowned sparrow is the aristocrat of his family. But besides all this he lacks the yellow seen on the head of the white-throat, and the

median white-crown stripe that separates the two
black lines is broader than in the white-throat.
His chin, too, is less markedly white.

The song of the two sparrows is entirely different. The white-throat's is a plaintive whistle, both
rich and sweet, while the white-crowned has a
comparatively low, commonplace song, something
like —

whe - he - he - he - hee - hĕ

LVII.

FIELD SPARROW; BUSH SPARROW.

MR. BURROUGHS calls the bush sparrow chippy's "country cousin," and when you have once
seen him you will agree that no detail could describe him as well. Instead of having a smooth
tight fitting coat, his feathers are ruffled up care-
lessly while the clear ashy breast of chippy is replaced by a rusty one, and his cap is much duller.
Altogether his appearance is thoroughly rustic.
But he has not only these external marks of the
country cousin. Chippy is eminently sophisti-
cated, and assumes "airs," and indulges in petulance that is foreign to the kindly sparrow race.
The little bush sparrow, however, is a pleasing
contrast. He has a genuine, simple nature, and

when he sings his sweet song wins your friendship
on the spot. But he has one habit that exasper-
ates an observer. There is a field of low bushes
on the north side of " Paradise," and I have chased
after him through it until I quite forgot that he
had any virtues! No sooner would I hear his
song, catch a glimpse of a brown back, and creep
up softly within opera-glass range, than lo! there
he would be hopping about singing from a bush a
rod away!

LVIII.

FOX SPARROW.

In the spring of 1887 the fox sparrows were
here for some time, coming occasionally to eat
buckwheat on the corn boxes with the tree sparrows and juncos. They were large, fat birds,
strikingly bluish-slate about the head, and rich
reddish-brown on the wings, lower part of back,
and tail. The centres of the breast markings
were set in an ochraceous suffusion.

They came to the boxes much more timidly
than the other birds, slipping in quietly for a few
mouthfuls, as if afraid of being seen. But they
made themselves at home in the saplings on the
edge of the woods right back of the house, singing
in the sun quite fearlessly, even when I was walking about on the crust, staring at them through

my glass, and taking liberties with their mother tongue. Their song resembled that of the song sparrow in arrangement of note, but was richer, and had a plaintive cast.

LIX.

BROWN CREEPER.

At last we have a bird to put into our empty pigeon-hole, No. 2, — the "creepers." Like the "thrashers and wrens" in No. 10, his prevailing color is brown, and he has a long slender bill, while he resembles the nuthatch — his neighbor in No. 12 — in habits. In his way, however, the brown creeper is a unique bird. He is so nearly the color of the brown bark of the trees you often overlook him as he goes rocking up their sides. When pecking at the bark he looks even more *convex* than the yellow hammer; for besides the curve given by his tail as he braces himself by it, and the continuing curve of his back as he bends forward, his bill is long and curved, thus completing the arc.

He is a systematic workman, going over his ground in a painstaking fashion, sometimes even flitting back a few feet to examine a piece of moss over again. He usually begins at the bottom of a tree and works up, sometimes circling, at others flitting up, and again rocking straight up the side. He nests as close to the heart of the tree as he can get, little brown wood sprite that he is, creeping under a bit of loosened bark, or getting into some cranny of the sort, that he can fit up for his white eggs with felt and feathers.

WARBLERS.

When you begin to study the warblers you will probably conclude that you know nothing about birds, and can never learn. But if you begin by recognizing their common traits, and then study a few of the easiest, and those that nest in your locality, you will be less discouraged; and when the flocks come back at the next migration you will be able to master the oddities of a larger number. They belong in pigeon-hole No. 9, — labelled " wood warblers," and are a marked family.

Most of them are very small — much less than half the size of a robin — and are not only short but slender. Active as the chickadee or kinglet, they flit about the trees and undergrowth after insects, without charity for the observer who is trying to make out their markings. Unlike the waxwing, whose quiet ways are matched by its subdued tints, or the uniformly coated kinglets or the greenlets in the pigeon-hole next to them, as a group, the warblers are dashed with all the glories of the rainbow, a flock of them looking as if a painter's palette had been thrown at them. You can see no philosophy or poetry in the bewildering combinations, and when you find that they differ entirely with age and sex, you despair of ever knowing them.

Why they should be called warblers is a puzzle, as a large percentage of them have not as much song as chippy — nothing but a thin chatter, or a shrill piping trill. If you wish a negative conception of them, think of the coloring and habits of the cuckoo. No contrast could be more complete. The best places to look for them during migration are young trees, orchards, and sunny slopes. Here I find them in old orchards, swamps, the raspberry patch, and the edge of the woods. In Northampton they showed an annoying fondness for pine-tree tops, but atoned for it by giving us the best views of them in the orchards and on the steep bank of Mill River.

LX.

SUMMER YELLOW-BIRD; GOLDEN WARBLER; YELLOW WARBLER.

If you have caught glimpses of this little warbler building in your orchard or the shrubbery of your garden, you may have wondered about his relation to the other yellow-bird — the goldfinch. But when you look at them critically you will find the two entirely distinct. The goldfinch dons a bright canary suit, set off by black cap, wings,

and tail. The summer yellow-bird, on the contrary, wears heavier yellow, and is not only without the contrasting black, but looks dull from the
" obsolete " brown streaks on his vest. The goldfinch is a larger bird, and, as he lives on seeds
rather than insects, has the thick finch bill instead
of the fine one of the warbler. On the wing, at
a distance, the peculiar curved undulating flight
of the goldfinch marks him; and when you are
near enough to hear him sing, you will find that
his canary-like song is totally unlike the warbler
trill of the summer yellow-bird.

One spring we discovered a golden warbler's
nest in the top of an apple-tree in the old Northampton orchard, near the nest a song sparrow had
built at the bottom of a brush heap, and the loose
bunch of twigs the catbirds had patched up with
newspaper in an apple-tree crotch. Perhaps the
little bird thought its persistent enemy, Madam
Cowbird, would be less likely to visit its nest if
other mother birds were on the watch near by —
for the golden warbler is the bird spoken of as
having had to build three stories to rid itself of
the cowbird's eggs.

LXI.

REDSTART.

THE long tail of the redstart makes him appear
about the size of a chipping bird. In habits,

however, he is more like the flycatchers than the
sparrows. Indeed, you might imagine that it was
from his flycatcher-like way of starting up or falling through the air unexpectedly that he got his
name ; for then you can see the blotches of rich
salmon that mark his wings and tail. However
this may be, the rest of his plumage is as striking
as his tail. His back is glossy black, and each
side of his white breast is ornamented with a
patch of bright salmon or red. The female, as
usual, is plainer than her spouse — has no black
on her breast, is olivaceous above, and light yellow where the male is salmon. The young birds
are like their mother, only browner above. As
the young males begin to put in coat or vest a
patch or a gore of their father's colors, they get
a ludicrously motley look ; and when they finally
come out in the full handsome suit of black and
red, you imagine them as proud as the college
senior with his silk hat.

Like the flycatchers, the redstarts are fluffy
birds and sit with drooping wings. But they
show warbler blood by the mad way they career
about, opening and shutting their tails fan-fash-
ion, turning somersaults, flitting from branch to
branch, stopping a second to give a little burst of
song, and then fluttering around again ; chasing
helter-skelter among the bushes ; and suddenly
falling through the leaves as if they had been shot,
only to snap up their prey and dart off to begin
their gambols over again.

They are winning, friendly little things, and make pretty nests of fine roots, birch bark, and flower cotton, or some such dainty material. According to individual taste, they build in apple-tree crotches, low roadside bushes, or in saplings

in open woods. In "Paradise" one once built in a loop of grape-vine by the river, and when her gray nest was nearly finished she had a pretty way of sitting inside and leaning over the edge to smooth the outside with her bill and neck, as if she were moulding it. The redstarts take good care to select bark the color of the tree, and in that way defy any but the keenest scrutiny. A little housewife will sometimes fly to her nest with strips of bark four inches long streaming from her bill.

The redstart's song is a fine, hurried warbler

trill that he accents on the end as if glad it was done.

Te - ka - te - ka - te - ka - te - ka - teek'.

One morning as I was watching a young hairy woodpecker, the solicitude of a redstart diverted me. Keeping up a nervous, worried cry, she eyed me from all sides, and when I moved, followed me in such a significant way that when I had looked through the crotches for her nest without finding it, I concluded the young were out. Father Redstart, — a young male with the scarlet just appearing on the sides of his breast, — meanwhile, showed about as much paternal anxiety as Mr. Indigo on similar occasions. Suddenly I espied one of the baby birds, a wee scrawny, gray thing, sitting on the dead branch of a fallen tree. As I came near him, his mother's terror was pitiful. She flew about as if distraught ; now trying to draw me away, she cried out and fluttered her wings beseechingly; then, finding that I still kept looking toward the little fellow, she flew down between us and tried to lure me off. I was very anxious to see if she would " trail," and so was merciless. Walking toward her trembling bird I raised my hand as if to take him, at the same time glancing over at her — behold ! she was trying another device — assuming indifference, as if divining that my interest in her was greater than in her little one. Her eyes were fixed on me, however, and just before the baby flew from my approaching hand, she dashed down and flew about wildly, trailing, as I had hoped. It was pitiful to see her distress, and having taken a good look at her I retreated as fast as possible.

Each bird has its own method of decoy: the whippoorwill starts up the leaves that look like her scampering babies; the kingfisher falls on the surface of the water; and the redstart, instead of spreading her wings and tail and dragging them on the ground as the oven-bird does, spreads and drags her tail, while she flutters her wings with a tremulous motion, which is much more effective, — suggestive of weakness and helplessness to the hungry animal, who finds a fat, full-grown bird more appetizing than a scrawny youngster; suggestive of anguish to the man, to whom it seems an appeal for mercy. The love of knowledge gave little excuse for treating a poor little mother to such a scare, but I consoled myself by thinking that she would be all the more wary when real danger threatened.

LXII.

BLACK AND WHITE CREEPING WARBLER.

As his name indicates, this creeper is entirely black and white. Except on the underside of his breast, where there is an area of plain white, the colors are arranged mostly in alternate streaks. Although much more slender, the creeper is just about the length of the chickadee, of whom he re-minds you by his fondness for tree trunks and branches. His habits of work, though, are much more suggestive of the nuthatch and brown creeper, and as the three are often found together during migration, it is easy to compare them.

The black and white creeper is more active than the others; that is, he has more of the restless warbler habit of flitting. He is not as painstak-ing nor as systematic as the brown creeper; and has neither as good head nor feet as the nuthatch. Where the brown creeper would go over a tree trunk twice, to be sure that nothing had escaped him, the black and white creeper will run up the side of a trunk a little way, then bob about on the branches for a moment, and flit off to another tree. He will hang head down from a branch to peck at the bark, and circle round a small tree horizontally, but I have never seen him go down a tree head first, as the nuthatch does, or walk around the underside of a branch. He will stand and look over the edge of a branch as if trying to see around underneath, but if he concludes to go to the other side he will flit around instead of walking. His song is a high-keyed trill, and as he is protected by being nearly the color of the gray bark he is usually clinging to, it is a grate-ful help to the discovery of his whereabouts.

LXIII.

BLACKBURNIAN WARBLER; HEMLOCK WARBLER; ORANGE-THROATED WARBLER.

THE Blackburnian is one of the handsomest and most easily recognized of the warblers. His throat is a rich orange or flame color, so brilliant that it is enough in itself to distinguish him from any of the others. His back is black with yellowish markings. His crown is black, but has an orange spot in the centre ; and the rest of his head, except near his eye, is the same flaming orange as his throat. His wings have white patches, and his breast is whitish, tinged with yellow. His sides are streaked with black. The female and young are duller, the black of their backs being mingled with olive ; while their throats are yellow instead of orange.

Now and then you are fortunate enough to get a near view of this exquisite bird, but he has an exasperating fondness for the highest branches of the tallest trees. You can see there is something up there, but as you throw your head back and strain through your opera-glass, you fancy it is some phantom bird flitting about darkening the leaves. The seconds wear into minutes, but you dare not move. Your glasses don't help you to see through the leaves, but you feel sure that something will appear in a moment, over the edge

of that spray or on the end of that bare twig, and
it won't do to miss it. So when your neckache
becomes intolerable you fix your eyes immovably
on the most promising spot, and step cautiously
backward till you can lean against a tree. The
support disappoints you, your hand trembles as
much as ever, and your neck is growing stiff. You
make a final effort, take your glass in both hands,
and change your focus, when suddenly a low, fine
trill that you recognize from being accented on
the end like a redstart's, comes from a branch several feet higher than before over your head. Your
neck refuses to bend an inch more. You despair.
But all at once your tormentor comes tumbling
through the leaves after an insect that has gotten
away from him, and you catch one fleeting glimpse
of orange that more than repays you for all your
cramps.

LXIV.

BLACK-THROATED BLUE WARBLER.

LIKE other ladies, the little feathered brides
have to bear their husbands' names, however inap-
propriate. What injustice! Here an innocent
creature with an olive-green back and yellowish
breast has to go about all her days known as the
black-throated blue warbler, just because that
happens to describe the dress of her spouse! The
most she has in common with him is a white spot

on her wings, and that does not come into the name at all. Talk about woman's wrongs! And the poor little things cannot even apply to the legislature for a change of name!

You do not blame them for nesting in the mountains and the seclusion of northern woods, to get away from the scientists who so ignore their individuality. For in this case it is not their mates who are at fault. They are as pleasing, inoffensive birds as any in the warbler family, and go about singing their *z-ie* guttural as they hunt over the twigs and branches, without the slightest assumption of conjugal authority.

Indeed, I saw one last August suing very humbly for his little lady's favor. She was either out of temper, or else inclined to coquette with him. He would fly to her side in a prettily gentle, unobtrusive way, but she would not even sit on the same branch with him. Off she would go to the next tree. And he would meekly follow after!

The blue-back has a pretty way of turning up his head for a look before he flies to the branch above him, or clambering about by the help of a stem here, or the side of a sapling there, for, as Mr. Burroughs says, he is not a gymnast. He is a winning, trustful little bird, and will often stop his work as you come by, to look at you.

LXV.

YELLOW-RUMPED WARBLER; MYRTLE WARBLER.

DURING migration the yellow-rumped is one of the. most abundant warblers. It is a hardy, robust-looking bird; the first of the family to appear in the spring, and one of the last to leave in the fall. You can recognize an adult male very easily in spring, because the black zouave jacket he wears over his white vest has conspicuous white and yellow side pieces.

The yellow-rump is a fearless bird, and frequents undergrowth as well as tree tops, so, if you can induce an adult male to keep still long enough on a spring morning, you will readily note the yellow crown that sets off his slaty-blue back, and the white chin that gives the effect of a choker. The adult female is dressed in much the same way, but is duller, and offers less marked contrasts in color. In the winter, like many other birds, they are both much altered — above they are washed with umber brown, and below, a paler wash of the same obscures their summer markings.

Sometimes you will see large flocks of the yellow-rumped without any other warblers, but as a general thing you will discover a few other species, and sometimes there will be a dozen different kinds together. The myrtle warbler has a coarse

z-ie call, and a trill that is heavier than that of
the golden warbler.

LXVI.

CHESTNUT-SIDED WARBLER.

WHEN I first saw the chestnut-sided warbler
he was flitting about the upper branches of the
saplings in the raspberry patch, about three rods
away, and I put down his yellow cap and wing
bars as white, and did not even see the chestnut
bands along his sides. I noted his pure white
breast, however, and his loud, cheerful *whee-he-
he*, so strikingly unlike the ordinary warbler trill
or the *z-ie* tones of some species. The next day,
after looking him up and finding what ought to
be there, I discovered, by the help of my glasses,
what, in fact, seemed little more than a maroon
line beside the wings. But in a few days I found
another bird whose chestnut sides were as the
books would have them, and I felt like shouting
Eureka!

Though I could not detect the nests that should
have been in the saplings bordering the clearing,
I found plenty of mother chestnuts leading their
broods about. They were among the pleasantest
acquaintances of the summer. Such charming little birds as they are!

My first hint of what was going on was the
sight of one of the dainty little ladies peering at

me from under the leaves and twigs, with a mouthful of worms. After hunting through the low bushes for some time, I ferreted out some bird's baby, a grayish mite with light wing bars, and wavy shadowy markings across its breast. But it was not until the next day that I had proof that it belonged to my bird. While watching some vireos in the bushes just in the edge of the clearing, the mother suddenly appeared. Perking up her tail and drooping her wings, she leaned over so as to be able to see me, gave a few little questioning smacks, and then flew down into the bush only a few feet from me, and fed the little bird without fear.

Fear seems to be an instinct, an inheritance with her, but her own confidence is strong enough to conquer it. Indeed, she is altogether sensible, straightforward, industrious, and confiding — a captivating, motherly body.

LXVII.

MARYLAND YELLOW - THROAT; BLACK - MASKED GROUND WARBLER.

IF your walks lead you through low underbrush, weed-grown river banks, alder swamps, or other rough, damp places, you will very likely notice the loud, quick *wheé - che-tee*, *wheé-che-tee*, *wheé-che-tee* that betrays the Maryland yellow-

throat. He is often shy and you may follow his
voice for a long time and not get a glimpse of
the bird, but see him once and you will never forget the picture. You will find him hopping about
either on the ground or near it, for he is truly a
ground warbler.

His back is olive-green, with the chin, throat,
and breast rich yellow. The forehead is black,
and there is a peculiar, mask-like, oblong black
patch on each side of his face that extends from
the bill back to the neck, and is separated from
the dark part of the head by a strip of ash. The
colors of the female are much duller, as she lacks
the black patch and the bright yellow.

If you would see the Maryland yellow-throat
at his best, you must invade the dense tangle of
an alder swamp, so often the fugitive's last ref-
uge, where you can get only mosaic glimpses of
blue sky overhead, and cannot distinguish a person twenty feet away; where you must push
through the interwoven boughs, picking your
steps around bogs, over slippery logs and tree
trunks, where luxuriant growths of wild grape-
vine, clematis, and the clinging galium beautify
the sturdy alders; where the royal fern, stretching above your waist, flowers in obscurity.

Here, in this secure cover, our little friend
seems to lose his timidity and blossoms out in the
full beauty of his nature. We find him singing to
himself as he runs over the alder boughs, exam-

ining the leaves with the care of a vireo, or clambering down the side of an alder stalk to hunt at its roots. *Whr-r-ree'-chee-tee, whr-r-ree'-chee-tee, whr-r-ree'-chee-tee*, the cheery rich song comes vibrating through the air, to be echoed from the far-off corners of the swamp. We sit down on an old moss-covered log to eat our lunch, and in answer to my call the sociable little warbler comes nearer and nearer till at last he catches sight of us. With what charming curiosity he peers down at us! What can be his thoughts of the strange intruders as he takes a half circle to inspect us, first from one point and then from another!

A little further along I come upon a father bird who is even more friendly. He is feeding his hungry little ones, and goes about in a most business-like way hunting for food, but still takes time for an occasional warble. He sees me, but, after a casual survey, keeps on with his work with the calmness of preoccupation, answering my call in a naïve, off-hand manner that is very gratifying.

LXVIII.

THRUSHES.

AFTER spending a morning with a flock of warblers, trying to fix your glass on the spot overhead where the leaves stirred, striving to catch the colors of the cap and wing bars of the

little object fluttering through the branches of a
sapling three or four rods away; making your
neck ache looking for the vexatious flitters that
hunt in the tops of the highest trees; following
the hint of a faint *chip* here, while you keep your
eye on half a dozen of the rarer warblers that
have just come in sight over there; losing track
of the whole flock as you stop to study the habits
of one; and then having to trudge the woods
over, straining your ears till convinced that you
are deaf, as you try in vain to catch the *chick-
a-dee-dee* of the titmouse, or the *yang, yang* of
the nuthatch, which would give a clue to the
whereabouts of their companions, the runaways
— after a morning spent in this way, you will
come back to the thrushes with a feeling of pos-
itive relief.

In the first place, they are large enough to be
seen, and give you the full benefit of their size
by keeping near the ground. Then, if you find
one, he is likely to stay and let you inspect him.
Moreover, it is possible to identify him without
knowing about each individual tail feather and
wing marking. Besides all this, you gain self-
respect in associating with the thrushes. When
you have chased after a flock of warblers half a
day, only to find, on comparing your notes with
descriptions in the books, that what you saw
applies equally well to three or four widely dif-
fering species, your opinion of yourself dwindles

unpleasantly; depressing doubts creep into your
mind. But with the thrushes the case is reversed.
You can write essays in your note-book while they
sit and look at you. You can arrange their songs
in flats and sharps to suit your fancy, and they
will not demur.

Doubtless, you must treat them with respect.
But whoever thought of making a noise in the
presence of a philosopher, or taking liberties with
a sage? You feel flattered by being allowed to
watch them at a distance, and when you get home
and find Ridgway's Manual ready to indorse your
identifications, your self-respect is restored.

With the thrushes, our pigeon-holes are filled,
and it will be well to glance over their labels
again before leaving them : No. 1, flycatchers ;
No. 2, crows, jays, etc. ; No. 3, blackbirds, orioles,
etc. ; No. 4, sparrows, finches, etc. ; No. 5, tanagers; No. 6, swallows; No. 7, waxwings, etc. ; No.
8, vireos ; No. 9, wood warblers ; No. 10, wrens,
thrashers, etc. ; No. 11, creepers ; No. 12, nuthatches and titmice ; No. 13, kinglets, etc. ; No.
14, thrushes, etc. What a contrast between the
birds in the first hole and those in the last —
what a distance between the bony, awkward flycatchers, with their undeveloped voices, and the
shapely dignified thrushes, the nightingales of
America !

But in their order, the birds of most of the
pigeon-holes show some obvious, external relation

to those in the hole above them. The flycatchers, like the crows and jays, are songless birds; the crows and jays are similar to the blackbirds and orioles in build and habit; the blackbirds and orioles are linked with the sparrows and finches by the short, conical-billed bobolink and cowbird; the sparrows and finches resemble the tanagers in general build; the swallows in No. 6 seem to stand alone; but the waxwings resemble the vireos in elegance and tone of plumage; the vireos approach the wood warblers in size and form; and while there is a natural gap between Nos. 9 and 10, as two families are omitted, the wrens and thrashers are like the creepers in shape of bill and general coloring; and the creeper is closely connected with the nuthatch of No. 12, nuthatches and titmice, while the titmice in their turn show the nearness of the family to the kinglets. These resemblances, however, are mostly superficial, not real.

The several thrushes are so closely allied that there is difficulty in discriminating between them, and I confess they puzzled me at first. I began by studying the wood, the hermit, and the tawny. These three all had brown backs, white speckled breasts, and beautiful voices. But before long I found they could be easily distinguished by variations in the shade of brown on their backs, by size and arrangement of the speckles, and by the quality of their songs.

Coloring of Back.

The brown of the *wood* thrush is reddest on head and shoulders.

The brown of the *hermit* is reddest on the tail.

The *tawny* has a uniformly tawny back.

Speckling of Breast.

The *wood* is heavily speckled with large brown spots, except on a plain middle area.

The *hermit*, in keeping with his smaller size, is less heavily marked, with smaller speckles, and has a plain area underneath, as well as on his neck and breast.

The *tawny* is only lightly spotted on the sides of his breast, and has a tawny chin and throat.

Character of Song.

The *wood* has a loud, rich, broken song.

The *hermit's* resembles the wood's in quality, but is much superior. It has a trill inserted in each phrase.

The *tawny* has a low sweet song consisting of a succession of trills, in descending scale.

In many places the wood thrush is found in the most open ground, and the hermit in the densest forest, but this is not always the case.

The most remarkable of the groups of sweet-voiced birds, the thrushes, are perhaps the most completely protected, for they are not only inconspicuous in coloring and of quiet habits, but seek the shelter of the forest for a home.

LXIX.

WILSON'S THRUSH; VEERY; TAWNY THRUSH.

IN Northampton, I have heard the veery sing
in the orchard by the river, where the catbird, the
song sparrow, the yellow warbler, and the redstart
nested, and where the cuckoo, the rose - breasted
grosbeak, the yellow-throated vireo, and flocks of
migrating warblers came to call. There it was
that the catbird tried to imitate the Wilson's
song. Perhaps the indignity drove the thrush on
to " Paradise " — in any case, he made his home
there, choosing the most beautiful places to sing
in, and hopping about among the ferns over the
pine needles that matched the soft brown of his
coat.

How well I remember spending one Sunday
afternoon in the pine grove, sitting where the
ground was strewn with glistening needles, and
leaning against a rugged pine trunk flecked by
the sunlight. And how when the symphony of
wind spirits softly touching their harp strings
in the tree tops had soothed every sense into rest
and peace, across the grove, from the trees on
the hillside and the bushes by the river in anti-
phonal chorus, rang out the low trilling chant of
the veeries.

Here, at home, I know one Wilson's thrush
that sings in a locust-tree close to a house by the

side of the road, apparently indifferent to the baying of hounds, as well as the noisy play of the children ; but I have also found others that were shy, even in the seclusion of an alder swamp.

In our woods there are five haunts of the veery. Two are in a dry second growth, one of which is on the western exposure of the woods where the coldest winds sweep over the hill, and little is heard save the woodpecker's reveille and the pensive note of the wood pewee. Here the thrushes' chief occupation is to turn the dry leaves aside with their bills, and scratch among them, oven-bird fashion, for worms. The three other places are moist ferneries, two of them being in the most protected part of the woods. One is in the partridges' cover, the grove of maple saplings where the redstart and the oven-bird nest, and the sun streams in to light up great masses of the arching hairy mountain fern, and warm the moss-covered drumming log of the partridge. Another is an old swamp on whose border a giant hemlock stands. Here the red morning sunlight creeps up soon after the birds are awake, and touches caressingly the smooth trunks of the beeches. It always seems as if the veery were more sociable here than on the dark western side of the woods. If you find one running along on the dark moss, you are sure to see another standing among the ferns ; if you stop to see how the sunlight shimmers through the young hemlocks, a friendly *kree-ah* from a bush near by will prepare you for the low song that trills in descending scale through the cool morning air, and breaks the hush of sunrise, as one after another of the peaceful songsters takes it up and carries it along.

In this swamp, on the soft decayed wood in the top of an old stump, five or six feet from the ground, one of the veeries' nests was found, and I think that careful search might have revealed others. But although such places seem best suited to their tastes, I have found a nest in a locality as dissimilar as could be imagined. It was on the edge of a raspberry patch where the sun beat down nearly all day long. The nest was deserted when I found it. Such a pretty structure as it was! Within a foot or so of the ground, wedged in between the sides of a young beech, it was made almost entirely of old leaves, and completely disguised by the crisp brown ones still clinging to the twigs. The lining was of dead leaves, roots, and stems. The four eggs were a beautiful, unspotted, robin's-egg blue. What a pity it seemed that such an attractive little home should be broken up! Who will ever know its tragedy! Perhaps the lonely father bird still haunts the woods mourning for his little mate!

In his own quiet way, the veery is a peculiarly sociable bird. So, although his song is the least remarkable of the three thrushes, his conversational notes and calls are both varied and numerous. His regular song is a series of trills descending the scale, and may be rendered as a trilled *trea, trea, trea.* Another form of this is *tree, tree, trum, rea, rea.*

Last spring I was greatly puzzled by hearing in the woods what seemed like the bleating of a lamb ; and although I soon suspected its source, it was some time before I *saw* the veery making this peculiar sound. It resembles a bleat so nearly that it can be fairly represented by the syllables *ba-ah-ah.* Mr. Brewster says it is a common note from the mountains of North Carolina to Maine and Labrador. I have heard it modified into a rapid run resembling *titaree.* As far as I have observed, this bleating call is usually connected with flight, or motion of some kind.

The commonest calls of the veery when undisturbed are *kree-ah* and *kree-up.* His *kree'-whee-a* is in a higher key and suggests alarm. One day I went through the bushes where a family of young were hiding. The mother sat on a branch looking down whisking her tail in dismay. *Whee-ah!* she called, and then added in undertone what seemed to be a warning, and sounded like *be still, be still!*

Sitting on a stump in the raspberry patch, I have drawn a number of veeries about me by imitating their *kree-ah,* and one of the rarest forest concerts I ever listened to began with this call.

It was on a June afternoon, when the sunbeams slanted lazily through the heavy summer air, tipping the fern fronds, and giving a touch of golden enchantment to the brown leaves that strewed the ground. *Kree-ah, kree-up*, came the sweet, rich call, first from one side and then another, till a dozen thrushes gathered. Then from their leafy covers rose the grave beautiful song. It seemed the choral of a dream, in which each note came forth as an inspiration.

LXX.

HERMIT THRUSH.

In literature and in the field the tawny and hermit thrushes are constantly confounded. The most marked differences have been given, but there are a few lesser points that may be of use in distinguishing them. The back of the hermit is olive, while the tawny, as his name indicates, has a tawny back. The hermit has the habit of raising his tail and then letting it drop straight down, while the tawny raises his tail higher, and lowers it only to the horizontal. The hermit is shy and solitary; the tawny sociable and comparatively confiding. The veery nests in various places; the hermit, almost always on the ground in a swamp, where he builds with leaves, sedges, and moss.

The call of the tawny is greatly varied, but the
hermit has a peculiar, nasal *chuck*, which, Mr.
Bicknell says, suggests " the note of a distant
blackbird."

The low, sweet, trilled song of the tawny bears
little resemblance to the loud, richly modulated
song of the hermit; but as they have been mistaken for each other, it may be well to give the
approximate relations of time and note in musical phrase. Like the song of the tawny, the
hermit's is divided into three parts, going down
the scale. But the trill is, here, only the middle
of each phrase

Variations from this occur in broken songs, as:

ah re oo-oo,

At a little distance this is probably the most
beautiful song of our woods. Mr. Burroughs
says that to him it is the finest sound in nature.
In the Adirondack region the retiring hermit is
appropriately known as the " swamp angel."

On the beautiful May morning when we found
the red-winged blackbirds " fluting their *o-ka-lee*"
over the field of cowslips, we went on to the woods
back of the alder swamp where the wild flowers

were blossoming. Pushing up through the dead leaves hundreds of yellow adder tongues turned back their petals and darted out their red stamens; colonies of spring beauties were springing up in the woods, raising their tiny pearl stems, spreading out their two slender green leaves, and opening their delicate crowning cups of pure white or delicate rose. At the foot of the tree trunks clusters of "ladies and gentlemen," — "squirrels' corn," some call them — looked from their luxuriant cover of green leaf filaments. And close to the ground lay the children's shining red fungus "cups and saucers" to light up the woods. But in the midst of all this mute loveliness the minstrel of the forest came to sing for the flowers their lay of the spring. Sitting almost motionless on the dead branch of a fallen tree top, the thrush poured forth his *oh'-tir-a-lee-lee* in ever varying tone and melody, till the woods seemed enriched by the marvellous song.

Each bird seems to voice some phase of nature. The bobolink sings for the sunny meadow, the vireo for the shaded tree top, the goldfinch for the blue sky, the indigo - bird for the passing breezes, and the whippoorwill for the night; but the hermit thrush chants the forest Te Deums for sunrise and sunset. Ever since I was a child, in the long summer evenings we have walked through the woods to "William Miller Hill," to see the sunset and listen to the hermit's vespers.

As we went along, watching the red light slant across the trunks of the trees, we would sometimes be thrilled with his song, but not till we had reached the brow of the hill overlooking the village in the valley, and the dark line of wooded hills beyond, not till —

> " The golden lighting of the sinking sun
> O'er which clouds are brightening " —

had all melted away, the sun dropped behind the dark hills, and the rosy cloudlets training across the sky had gradually disappeared ; not till the afterglow of the sunset was turning to pale serene light, would the song of the hermit stir us with its full richness and beauty. Then from the wooded hillside it would come to us, filling the cool evening air with its tremulous yearning and pathos, and gathering up into short waves of song the silent music of the sunset — nature's benison of peace.

APPENDIX.

PIGEON-HOLES FOR THE PERCHING BIRDS MENTIONED IN THIS BOOK.

No. 1.
Flycatchers.

Phœbe.
Kingbird.
Wood Pewee.
Least Flycatcher.
Great-crested Flycatcher.

No. 2.
Crows, Jays, etc.

Crow.
Blue Jay.

No. 3.
Blackbirds, Orioles, etc.

Crow Blackbird.
Bobolink.
Meadow-lark.
Oriole.
Red-winged Blackbird.
Cowbird.

No. 4.
Sparrows, Finches, etc.

Chippy.
Field Sparrow.
Tree Sparrow.
Song Sparrow.
Goldfinch.
White-throated Sparrow.
White-crowned Sparrow.
Fox Sparrow.
Indigo Bunting.
Purple Finch.
Junco.
Snowbird.
Chewink.
Rose-breasted Grosbeak.
Crossbills.

No. 5.
Tanagers.

Scarlet Tanager.

No. 6.
Swallows.

Barn Swallow.
Bank Swallow.
Cliff Swallow.

No. 7.
Waxwings, etc.

Cedar-bird.

No. 8.
Vireos.

Red-eyed Vireo.
Yellow-throated Vireo.
Warbling Vireo.

No. 9.
Wood Warblers.

Blackburnian Warbler.
Myrtle Warbler.
Black and White Creeping Warbler.
Black-throated Blue Warbler.
Golden Warbler.
Chestnut-sided Warbler.
Maryland Yellow-throat.
Oven-bird.
Redstart.

No. 10. Wrens, Thrashers, etc.	No. 11. Creepers.	No. 12. Nuthatches and Titmice.	No. 13. Kinglets.	No. 14. Thrushes, Bluebirds, etc.
Catbird. Brown Thrasher. Winter Wren.	Brown Creeper.	Chickadee. Nuthatch.	Ruby-crowned Kinglet. Golden-crowned Kinglet.	Robin. Bluebird. Wilson's Thrush. Hermit Thrush.

DRAWER.

Grouse.
Yellow-billed Cuckoo.
Black-billed Cuckoo.
Kingfisher.
Hairy Woodpecker.
Downy Woodpecker.
Yellow-bellied Woodpecker.
Red-headed Woodpecker.
Golden-winged Woodpecker.
Whippoorwill.
Night-hawk.
Swift.
Humming-bird.

GENERAL FAMILY CHARACTERISTICS OF BIRDS TREATED.

CUCKOOS.

Long slender birds whose breasts are whitish and backs brown, with a faint bronze lustre. Bill, long and curved. Call, loud and prolonged. Song, wanting. Habits, eccentric — strange silent birds, living in undergrowth or low trees.

KINGFISHERS.

Large top-heavy birds with long crests, slate-blue backs, and white breasts. Bill, very large and strong for holding fish. Flight, rapid and prolonged. Song, a loud hurried trill. Fishermen by occupation, they live about rivers and lakes, excavating nests in the banks.

WOODPECKERS.

Plumage, largely black and white. Bill, strong and long for drilling through bark and wood. Flight, noisy, flickering. Call, loud and shrill. Song, wanting, except as they drum on trees, etc. Habits, phlegmatic, most of time spent clinging, erect, to sides of tree trunks. (Exception, yellow hammer : plumage, brownish, instead of black and white ; song, a loud full trill ; habits, more like ground woodpeckers ; haunts ant-hills, fields, and fence-posts, etc.)

GOATSUCKERS.

Mottled brownish and grayish birds, with tiny bills and enormous mouths for catching insects on the wing. Nest, wanting — eggs laid on bare ground or leaves.

SWIFTS.

Sooty or blackish birds that live on the wing, never lighting except in chimneys, towers, or hollow trees where they roost and nest. Bills small, mouths large, as in the goatsuckers.

HUMMING-BIRDS.

Diminutive birds whose plumage shows brilliant metallic lustre. Bills, slender and elongated for reaching insects and nectar at bottom of flower tubes. Flight, rapid, darting.

FLYCATCHERS.

Dull, gray birds with big heads and shoulders. Males and females similar in plumage. Bills, hooked at end. Songless or with short song (wood pewee, three notes). Habits, hunt by lying in wait for insects and then springing at them with nervous spasmodic movements. (Exception, kingbird.) Largely silent and motionless when not watching for food.

CROWS AND JAYS.

Large conspicuous birds, with strong bill and claws. Songless but clamorous. Active and boisterous — especially the blue jay.

BLACKBIRDS AND ORIOLES.

Plumage, striking, black prominent. (Exception, meadowlark.) Females generally duller, and in some cases smaller than males. Bills and claws, strong ; bills, long and conical. (Exceptions, bobolink and cowbird, whose bills are short and conical.)

SPARROWS AND FINCHES.

Fine songsters. Bills, short, stout, cone-shaped, for cracking seeds.

Sparrows. — Comparatively small, dull-plumaged birds, with striped backs ; much the color of the ground and bushes on which they live — males and females similar.

Finches. — Bright-plumaged birds, females duller than males.

TANAGERS.

Shy, brilliantly-colored birds, with dull-plumaged wives. They build low, but hunt for worms and sing their loud swinging song mostly in the cover of tree tops.

SWALLOWS.

Small-billed, big-mouthed insect eaters. Not songless, yet without musical power. When not flying they often perch on telegraph wires and the ridge-poles of barns.

WAXWINGS.

Elegant, delicately-tinted birds. Usually silent and re-tiring. They practise among themselves amazing courtesy and gentleness.

VIREOS.

Small olive-green or gray-backed, white-breasted birds ; much the color of the lights and leaf tints they live among. Bills, long and slender for holding worms. Songs, loud and continuous, from their tree-top covers. Nests pensile and delicate.

WARBLERS.

Plumage, mostly variegated and brilliant. Females generally duller than males. Song, in many cases only a trill. Food, insects. Habits, nervous, restless.

WRENS AND THRASHERS.

Small and large birds that sing their brilliant songs secure in the protection of their inconspicuous brown or gray dress and the dense thickets or forest undergrowth they frequent. As they spend little time in flight their wings are short, but the long tails of the thrashers are of great use in helping them along from bush to bush.

CREEPERS.

Small obscure brown birds that spend their time creeping up and down tree trunks, from which they get their living and in which they nest. Bill long, slender and curved. Tails stiff and bristly for bracing them as they work — like the woodpeckers'.

NUTHATCHES AND TITS.

Small tree birds usually found together in flocks except when breeding.

Nuthatches. — Slate-blue-backed birds that walk sedately up and down tree trunks, and run along branches upside down, like flies.

Chickadees. — Fluffy grayish birds that flit among tree tops.

KINGLETS.

Small fluffy greenish birds that flit about the leaves of shrubbery and trees after insects. Songs remarkable.

THRUSHES

Brown-backed, white-breasted birds, size of robin, or smaller. Bills, long and slender, fitted for worm diet. Habits, phlegmatic ; pensive birds, fond of sitting motionless. Finest of American songsters.

ARBITRARY CLASSIFICATIONS OF BIRDS DESCRIBED.

I. BIRDS FOUND IN CERTAIN LOCALITIES.

1. *About or near houses.* — Robin, chipping sparrow, song sparrow, junco, chimney swift, crow blackbird, warbling vireo, yellow-bellied woodpecker, tree sparrow, brown creeper, oriole, phœbe, purple finch, chickadee, catbird, red-eyed vireo, nuthatch, humming-bird, barn swallow.

2. *In gardens and orchards.* — Catbird, bluebird, waxwing, cuckoo, oriole, kingbird, kinglets, humming-bird, warbling vireo, yellow-throated vireo, yellow-bellied wood-

pecker, purple finch, goldfinch, summer yellow-bird, warblers, cowbird, least flycatcher, yellow hammer.

3. *In fields and meadows.* — Meadow-lark, cowbird, nighthawk, crow, bank swallow, barn swallow, cliff swallow, vesper sparrow, field sparrow, bobolink, red-winged blackbird, snowflake, song sparrow.

4. *In bushes and clearings.* — White-throated sparrow, song sparrow, chipping sparrow, tree sparrow, field sparrow, white-crowned sparrow, junco, Maryland yellow-throat, kinglets, chewink, brown thrasher, rose-breasted grosbeak, catbird, robin, purple finch, goldfinch, winter wren.

5. *By streams and rivers.* — Phœbe, waxwing, bank swallow, kingfisher, yellow warbler, red-winged blackbird, Maryland yellow-throat, whippoorwill, barn swallow, bank swallow, cliff swallow.

6. *In woods.* — Thrushes, wood pewee, oven-bird, black and white creeper, woodpeckers, junco, nuthatch, grouse, great-crested flycatcher, chewink, whippoorwill, tree sparrow, fox sparrow, brown creeper, scarlet tanager, chickadee, Blackburnian warbler, crossbills, vireos, redstart, black-throated blue warbler, yellow-rumped warbler, winter wren.

7. *Edge of woods.* — Rose-breasted grosbeak, cowbird, redstart, wood pewee, woodpeckers, kingbird, cuckoo, oven-bird, bluebird, humming-bird, chickadee, chewink, great-crested flycatcher, brown thrasher, yellow-bellied woodpecker, tree sparrow, white-throated sparrow, white-crowned sparrow, fox sparrow, brown creeper, thrasher, vireos, oriole, purple finch, junco, warblers, yellow hammer, winter wren.

8. *Roadside fences.* — Bluebird, flicker, kingbird, red-headed woodpecker, goldfinch, white - crowned sparrow, field sparrow, vesper sparrow, song sparrow, white-throated sparrow.

9. *Thickets.* — White-throated sparrow, song sparrow, Maryland yellow-throat, chickadee, junco, chewink, brown thrasher, white-crowned sparrow, field sparrow, catbird,

Wilson's thrush, warblers (in migration), winter wren (in migration), chestnut-sided warbler.

10. *Pine woods.* — Warblers, kinglets, chickadee, brown thrasher, whippoorwill, white-crowned sparrow, crossbills, purple finch, nuthatch, woodpeckers.

II. Size compared with the Robin.

smaller than the robin.

1. *Less than half as large.* — Kinglets, chipping sparrow, goldfinch, chickadee, nuthatch, warblers, winter wren, least flycatcher, humming - bird, tree sparrow, field sparrow, brown creeper, yellow-throated vireo, warbling vireo.

2. *About half as large.* — Swift, red-eyed vireo, oven-bird, crossbills, wood pewee, purple finch, song sparrow, junco, indigo-bird.

3. *More than half as large.* — Phœbe, bluebird, waxwing, downy woodpecker, barn swallow, bank swallow, cliff swallow, vesper sparrow, white-crowned sparrow, fox sparrow, white-throated sparrow, bobolink, oriole, scarlet tanager, snow bunting.

about the same size as the robin.

Rose-breasted grosbeak, cowbird, red-headed woodpecker, hairy woodpecker, yellow - bellied woodpecker, chewink, great-crested flycatcher, red - winged blackbird, catbird, thrushes, kingbird.

larger than the robin.

Yellow hammer, kingfisher, crow, grouse, brown thrasher, whippoorwill, meadow-lark, cuckoo, night-hawk, keel-tailed blackbird, blue jay.

III. Colors.

COLORS STRIKING OR BRIGHT.

1. *Blue backs.* — Blue jay, bluebird (azure blue), nuthatch (slate-blue), kingfisher (slate-blue), indigo-bird, black-throated blue warbler, barn swallow (steel-blue).

2. *Chestnut or red breasts.* — Bluebird, robin, crossbills (male), scarlet tanager (male), chewink.

3. *Yellow or orange throats.* — Blackburnian warbler, Maryland yellow-throat, summer yellow-bird, yellow-throated vireo.

4. *Yellow or orange breasts.* — Yellow-throated vireo, summer yellow-bird, goldfinch, oriole, meadow-lark, Blackburnian warbler, Maryland yellow-throat.

5. *Red patch on top or back of head in males.* — Ruby-crowned kinglet, woodpeckers, kingbird.

6. *Red heads (entire head and neck red or madder pink).* — Red-headed woodpecker, purple finch (old males), crossbills (males).

7. *Birds wholly or largely black (males).* — Crow, blackbirds, cowbird, redstart (salmon patches on breast, wings, and tail), bobolink (whitish patches on nape of neck and back), rose-breasted grosbeak (carmine patch on breast, belly white), chewink (white breast, brown sides), oriole (orange below).

COLORS DULL OR PLAIN.

1. *Upper parts olive-green.* — Breast unspotted: Kinglets (patch of red or yellow in crown), vireos (top of head unmarked), tanager (female), crossbills (females). Breast spotted : Oven-bird (crown patch orange-brown bordered with black).

2. *Upper parts olive-gray.* — Cuckoos (tail very long, bill curved), great-crested flycatcher.

3. *Upper parts dusky grayish-olive.* — Phœbe (length about

seven inches), wood pewee (length about six inches), least flycatcher (length about five inches).

4. *Upper parts brown.* — *a.* Back without markings of any kind: Indigo-bird (female), brown thrasher (breast spotted, tail very long), Wilson's thrush (breast spotted, tail short), hermit thrush (breast spotted, tail short and red), winter wren (back barred).

b. Back more or less streaked: Meadow-lark (below yellow with black collar), female rose-breasted grosbeak (rose of male replaced by saffron yellow), bobolink (female and male in winter, buffish-yellow below), purple finch (female), brown creeper, grouse.

Sparrows: *c.* Breast unspotted in adult: Chipping (crown brick red), white-throated (yellow spot in front of eye), white-crowned (crown-cap of five lines), field sparrow (rusty look).

d. Breast spotted or streaked: Song (no white on tail), tree (breast with spot in centre, cap reddish).

5. *General color chiefly black and white.* — *a.* In large patches or areas: Snowflake, bank swallow, rose-breasted grosbeak (male), redstart (male), chewink (brown sides), red-headed woodpecker (head and neck red).

b. In stripes. Black and white creeper.

c. In spots (above, white below): Hairy woodpecker, downy woodpecker.

6. *Yellow band across end of tail.* — Waxwing (high crest).

7. *White band across end of tail.* — Kingbird (low crest).

8. *Crown and throat black (size small).* — Chickadee (back dull ash-gray).

9. *General color sooty.* — Chimney swift.

10. *General color slate.* — Catbird, junco (belly and outer tail feathers white).

BRILLIANT MALES CHANGING TO DULL COLORS OF FE-MALES IN AUTUMN.

Bobolink (becomes almost sparrowy in appearance), goldfinch (becomes flaxen-brown above and brownish-yellow below), scarlet tanager (becomes greenish-yellow), yellow-rumped warbler (becomes brownish).

BIRDS SHOWING WHITE ON TAIL FEATHERS IN FLIGHT.

Meadow-lark, vesper sparrow, junco, chewink (white triangles on corners of tail), rose-breasted grosbeak, several warblers, kingbird (white crescent bordering tail).

IV. Songs.

SINGERS.

1. *Particularly plaintive.* — Bluebird, white-throated sparrow, hermit thrush, meadow-lark, wood pewee.

2. *Especially happy.* — Bobolink, song sparrow, goldfinch, indigo-bird, chickadee.

3. *Short songs.* — Robin, chickadee, bluebird, Maryland yellow-throat, meadow-lark, great-crested flycatcher, whippoorwill, white-crowned sparrow.

4. *Long songs, with definite beginning, middle and end.* — Hermit thrush, indigo-bird, thrasher, chewink, song, field, tree, fox, white-crowned, and white-throated sparrows.

5. *Long songs, without definite beginning, middle, and end.* — Purple finch, catbird, goldfinch, warbling vireo.

6. *Long loud songs.* — Oriole, scarlet tanager, oven-bird, rose-breasted grosbeak, chewink, winter wren, brown thrasher.

TRILLERS.

(Saying *tee-ka-tee-ka-tee-ka*, or words to that effect.)

Low. — Redstart, summer yellow-bird, black and white creeper, junco, chippy, brown creeper, swift (saying *chippy-chippy-chirio*), nuthatch.

Loud. — Yellow hammer (*if–if–if–if–if–if–if*), kingfisher (alarm), oven-bird (saying *teacher*).

V. Peculiarities of Flight.

Conspicuously tail-steering : Keel-tailed blackbird.

Undulated flight: Goldfinch, woodpeckers, snowbird, blue-bird.

Circling flight : Swallows and night-hawks.

Labored flight : Bobolink, meadow-lark, sparrows.

Fluttering flight : Chimney swift.

Particularly direct flight : Robin, crow, keel-tailed black-bird, kingfisher, oriole, blue jay.

VI. Birds with Habit of Song-Flight.

Cowbird, bobolink, oven-bird, bluebird, kingbird, swift, woodpecker, red-shouldered blackbird, indigo - bird, song sparrow, Maryland yellow-throat, meadow-lark, kingfisher, cuckoo, goldfinch, night-hawk, purple finch.

VII. Marked Habits.

1. *Phlegmatic, meditative, fond of sitting quietly.* — Wax-wing, robin, thrushes, white-throated sparrow, meadow-lark, wood pewee, woodpeckers, swallows, kingfisher.

2. *Restless, constantly flitting about.* — Winter wren, king-lets, chickadee, warblers.

3. *Loquacious.* — Catbird, purple finch, crow blackbird, blue jay, red-eyed vireo, warbling vireo, oven-bird, swift, chippy, bobolink.

VIII. Birds that Walk instead of Hopping.

Keel-tailed blackbird, red-winged blackbird, crow,' par-tridge, cowbird, oven-bird, meadow-lark.

IX. Shape of Bill adapted to Food.

1. *Short and stout, for cracking seeds.* — Grosbeak, cross-bills (crossed for getting out spruce and pine seeds), purple finch, indigo-bird, junco, snow bunting, bobolink, sparrows, chewink.

2. *Long and slender for holding worms.* — Thrushes, warblers, orioles, kinglets, brown creeper.

3. *Hooked at end to hold insects.* — Vireos, flycatchers.

4. *Long and heavy for drilling holes in trees.* — Woodpeckers.

5. *Slender and delicate for reaching insects at bottom of flower tubes.* — Humming-bird.

6. *Large and long for holding fish.* — Kingfisher.

X. Where Certain Birds Nest.

1. *On the ground.* — Meadow-lark (meadows and fields), white - throated sparrow, partridge, snow bunting, nighthawk, bobolink, junco, oven-bird, song sparrow, hermit thrush, Maryland yellow-throat, black and white creeper, chewink, whippoorwill, vesper sparrow.

2. *In holes.* — *a.* Holes in trees and stubs: Woodpeckers, nuthatch, chickadee, bluebird, great-crested flycatcher.

b. Holes in river and other banks : Kingfisher, bank swallow.

3. *In orchards.* — Kingbird, goldfinch, waxwing, summer yellow-bird, chipping sparrow, catbird, robin, blue jay, redstart, cuckoo, least flycatcher.

4. *About houses, sheds, and barns.* — Robin, phœbe, eave swallow, chimney swift, bluebird (in knot - holes in out - houses or in bird boxes), chipping sparrow.

5. *In bushes.* — Cuckoo, chipping sparrow, catbird, rose-breasted grosbeak, red-eyed vireo, Wilson's thrush, red-winged blackbird, song sparrow, yellow warbler, indigo bunting, brown thrasher.

6. *In low trees.* — Tanager, chestnut-sided warbler, yellow warbler, redstart, red-eyed vireo, purple finch, kingbird, humming-bird, least flycatcher.

7. *In high trees.* — Robin, oriole (especially in elms), crow, crow blackbird, purple finch, vireos, wood pewee, Blackburnian warbler, crossbills, humming-bird.

8. *In other birds' nests.* — Cowbird, cuckoo (rarely).

9. *In crevices of logs or stumps.* — Winter wren.

10. *Under bark on trees.* — Brown creeper.

XI. Birds that are seen in Flocks when not Nesting.

Cedar-bird, night-hawk, bobolink, white-throated sparrow, junco, chickadee (small parties), nuthatch (small parties), blue jay (small parties), red-headed woodpecker, crossbill, purple finch, bluebird, goldfinch, kinglet, warblers, snowbird, blackbird, chimney swift, crow, swallows, vesper sparrow, tree sparrow, grouse.

BOOKS FOR REFERENCE.

A. O. U. Check-List of North American Birds, 1895, $2.00 ;
abridged edition, 25 cents. L. S. Foster, New York.

Audubon, John James. Birds of America ; Ornithological
Biography. (Both out of print.)

Baird, S. F., T. M. Brewer, and R. Ridgway. A History
of North American Birds. 5 vols. Little, Brown &
Co., Boston. $48.00.

Bendire, Chas. E. Life Histories of North American Birds.
2 vols. Smithsonian Institution, Washington. $15.00.

Chapman, Frank M. Handbook of Birds of Eastern North
America. D. Appleton & Co., New York. $3.00 ;
pocket edition, $3.50. Bird-Life. D. Appleton & Co.,
New York. $1.75. With colored plates, $5.00.

Coues, Elliott. Key to North American Birds. Dana Estes
& Co., Boston. $7.50.

Elliot, Daniel G. The Gallinaceous Game Birds of North
America. Francis P.. Harper, New York. $2.50.

Merriam, Florence A. Birds of Village and Field. Houghton, Mifflin & Co., Boston. $2.00.

Minot, H. D. The Land-Birds and Game-Birds of New
England. Second edition, edited by William Brewster.
Houghton, Mifflin & Co., Boston. $3.50.

Nehrling, Henry. Our Native Birds of Song and Beauty.
2 vols. George Brumder, Milwaukee. Unbound,
$16.00 ; bound, $18.00–$22.00.

Nuttall, Thomas. A Manual of the Ornithology of the
United States and Canada. (Out of print.) A Popular Handbook of the Ornithology of Eastern North
America, being a new edition of the Manual of Ornithology revised and annotated by Montague Chamber-
lain. 2 vols. Little, Brown & Co., Boston. $7.50.

Ridgway, Robert. A Manual of North American Birds. J. B. Lippincott Co., Philadelphia. $7.50.

Wilson, Alexander. American Ornithology. (Out of print.)

Wright, Mabel Osgood. Birdcraft. The Macmillan Co., New York. $2.50.

Wright, Mabel Osgood, and Elliott Coues. Citizen Bird. The Macmillan Co., New York. $1.50.

PERIODICALS.

Auk, The. A Quarterly Journal of Ornithology. Published for the American Ornithologists' Union by L. S. Foster, New York. $3.00 per annum.

Osprey, The. An Illustrated Monthly Magazine of Ornithology. The Osprey Company, New York. $1.00 per annum.

BOOKS CONTAINING ORNITHOLOGICAL ESSAYS AND SKETCHES.

Bolles, Frank. Land of the Lingering Snow ; At the North of Bearcamp Water ; From Blomidon to Smoky. Houghton, Mifflin & Co., Boston. $1.25 each.

Burroughs, John. Wake-Robin ; Winter Sunshine ; Birds and Poets ; Locusts and Wild Honey ; Pepacton ; Fresh Fields ; Signs and Seasons ; Riverby. Houghton, Mifflin & Co., Boston. $1.25 each.

Miller, Olive Thorne. Bird Ways ; In Nesting Time ; Little Brothers of the Air ; A Bird-Lover in the West ; Upon the Tree-tops. Houghton, Mifflin & Co., Boston. $1.25 each.

Robinson, Rowland E. In New England Fields and Woods. Houghton, Mifflin & Co., Boston. $1.25.

Torrey, Bradford. Birds in the Bush ; A Rambler's Lease ; The Foot-Path Way ; A Florida Sketch-Book ; Spring Notes from Tennessee ; A World of Green Hills. Houghton, Mifflin & Co., Boston. $1.25 each.

INDEX.